PENGUIN BOOKS
THE NAME OF MY BELOVED

Nikky-Guninder Kaur Singh was born in India, and went for high school to the USA. She received her BA in Philosophy and Religion from Wellesley College, her MA from the University of Pennsylvania, and her PhD from Temple University. She is currently Professor and Chair of the Department of Religious Studies at Colby College in Maine, USA. Her interests focus on poetics and feminist issues. Nikky Singh has published extensively in the field of Sikhism, including *The Feminine Principle in the Sikh Vision of the Transcendent* (Cambridge University Press, 1993). She has lectured widely in North America, England, France, India and Singapore, and her views have been aired on television and radio in America, Canada and India.

Dear Harpreet & Manpreet,

Always remember that
Waheguru is the Sole
Source of wordly Knowledge,
Wealth and happiness
with our blessings

24 June 06   Mom and Dad

VERSES OF THE SIKH GURUS

The Name of
My Beloved

Translated and introduced by
Nikky-Guninder Kaur Singh

With a foreword by Narinder Singh Kapany

PENGUIN BOOKS

Penguin Books India (P) Ltd., 11 Community Centre, Panchsheel Park, New Delhi 110 017, India
Penguin Books Ltd., 27 Wrights Lane, London W8 5TZ, UK
Penguin Putnam Inc., 375 Hudson Street, New York, NY 10014, USA
Penguin Books Australia Ltd., Ringwood, Victoria, Australia
Penguin Books Canada Ltd., 10 Alcorn Avenue, Suite 300, Toronto, Ontario, M4V 3B2, Canada
Penguin Books (NZ) Ltd., Cnr Rosedale & Airborne Roads, Albany, Auckland, New Zealand

First published in the United States by HarperCollins *Publishers* 1995
First published in India by Penguin Books India 2001

Copyright © Nikky-Guninder Kaur Singh 1995

10 9 8 7 6 5 4 3 2 1

Typeset in Palatino by Abha Graphics, New Delhi
Printed at Rekha Printers Pvt. Ltd., New Delhi

IN MEMORY OF MY PARENTS
IN WHOSE ARMS I FIRST HEARD THE GURUS' VERSE

Contents

Acknowledgements

I will always be indebted to my friend Kerry Brown for ushering me into the fascinating world of translation. She initially invited me to do an English version of Sikh scripture for the International Sacred Literature Trust published by HarperCollins, USA. I thank all my readers for their warm reception, and especially my students at Colby College who have intimately linked themselves with the temporally and spatially distant verses of the Sikh Gurus. During her world travels, my student Heather Miles even carried the book in her handbag, and during the 1999 graduation ceremonies, the College's valedictorian student, Will Polkinghorn, read Guru Nanak's 'Arati' in the Colby Chapel. It has been wonderful to communicate and share the divine passion of the Sikh Gurus with my western readership. My special thanks to Uncle Kapany of the Sikh Foundation in California, T. Sher Singh of the Centennial Foundation in Canada, and my childhood friend, Preety, in Chicago, for promoting my work in their own and special ways.

Since its first publication by HarperCollins, I have lost my father. Without parents, and without a home in Patiala, India seems even farther away. I miss the place where I first heard the verses of the Sikh Gurus. Their rhythm and power, stored in the deepest recesses of my psyche, resonate ever more strongly. I want to stay in touch with the soil and spirit in which I was born and nurtured.

I thank Penguin India for making my wish come true.

Nikky-Guninder Kaur Singh
Colby College, Waterville,
Maine 04901, USA.
May 13, 2001

Foreword

The founder of the Sikh religion, Guru Nanak, proclaimed his scriptures which later became the heart of the Guru Granth, dhur ki bani—the revealed Word. As one of the youngest major world religions, the Sikh faith retains the original manuscript of the scriptures intact to this day. But these scriptures do not only live on the printed page; they are also poetry set to music which lives as sacred sound in the everyday and special moments of the community's life. Perhaps most striking is the fact that the scriptures of the Sikhs include writings of numerous non-Sikh saints.

The Revelation was disseminated to the disciples in the language of the time and woven into the social, historic, political, folkloric, linguistic and mythological fabric of the day. Translation and interpretation of original religious scriptures into modern language is, thus, both a noble and a formidable task. In the words of Professor Puran Singh: "The poetic patina of the verbal vocabulary of Guru Granth does not necessarily have equivalencies or correspondences in the cross vocabulary of the English language." Herein lies the biggest challenge for a translator.

One of the earliest efforts to translate the Sikh scriptures into English was made by M. A. Macauliffe in 1909 in his monumental and widely acclaimed volumes *Sikh Religion*. His adoration and admiration of the Sikhs and the Sikh scriptures are best expressed in his statement: "All persons of discrimination acquainted with the Sikhs set a high value on them, but it appears that a knowledge throughout the world of the excellence of their religion would enhance even the present regard with which they are entertained."

Other Western scholars have imbibed the beauty and spirituality of the Sikh scriptures. Arnold Toynbee, after being exposed to translation of the Adi Granth (Guru Granth), proclaimed: "Mankind's religious future may be obscure, yet one thing can be foreseen: the living higher religions are going to influence each other more than before, in these days of increasing communication between all parts of the world and all branches of the human race. In this coming religious debate, the Sikh religion, and its scriptures, the Adi Granth will have something of special value to say to the rest of the world" (1960).

Pearl S. Buck studied the scriptures of great religions and came to this conclusion: "Shri Guru Granth Sahib is a source book, an expression of man's loneliness, his aspiration, his longings, his cry to God and his hunger for communication with that Being. I have studied the scriptures of other great religions, but I do not find elsewhere the same power of appeal to the heart and mind as I find in these volumes" (1960).

While numerous translations of Sikh scriptures have been undertaken in the past, the need for a translation of key sections of the Sikh scriptures into the language of today has been widely recognized. Dr Nikky-Guninder Kaur Singh, a young Sikh scholar of wisdom, dedication and zeal, has aptly undertaken this challenge. Daughter of the world class Sikh scholar and intellectual giant, Professor Harbans Singh, she has absorbed the beauty and spirituality of the Sikh scriptures from the cradle and developed her scholarly talents in the Western world. This publication is a testament to Nikky-Guninder Singh's love and adoration of the Sikh scriptures and her desire to share her ecstasy with Sikhs and non-Sikhs in the Western world. University and public libraries and, indeed, every Sikh household in the West should place this book on their shelves, and it should be required reading for all Sikh youth.

The International Sacred Literature Trust deserves to be specially commended for their commitment to the publication of translations of scriptures of various religions into modern and easily comprehensible language. Without the deep dedication, infinite persuasive powers and untiring efforts of the Executive Director, Kerry Brown, none of this would have been possible. Nor indeed without the commitment, efforts and scholarly precision of Dr W. Owen Cole, an old friend of the Sikh faith and a consulting editor with the ISLT.

The trustees of the Sikh Foundation are most gratified with the opportunity to sponsor this worthwhile project.

Narinder Singh Kapany
Chairman, The Sikh Foundation
15 June 1995

One Reality Is

The Guru Granth Sahib, the Sikh holy book, contains no historical narratives, no biographical details and no obligatory rituals. It is a collection of spiritually exalted poetry carrying only intimations. The theme running throughout is that of the individual's longing to experience the Transcendent Reality, moulded into poetic symbolism of great delicacy and beauty.

Granth means "book" and, since the Tenth and last human Guru declared it so in 1708, this collection of poetic revelations by the Sikh Gurus and by Hindu and Muslim saints has been treated by Sikhs as their personal Guru. The epithet *Sahib* is often added to the title as a sign of respect. It is also known as the *Adi Granth* or the "Primal Book". It is the sole visual and aural icon for the Sikhs and main source of their daily prayers. All rites of passage take place in the sound and sight of this text: the new-born baby is named in its presence, the marriage ceremony entails walking around it four times, death in a home is followed by a reading, often continuous, of its 1430 pages. In times of uncertainty and difficulty, or of joy and celebration, different types of recitations are the prescribed religious observance: saptah (seven-day), akhand (non-stop for forty-eight hours) or sampat (one particular hymn repeated after each different hymn).

The Name of My Beloved is a selection of poetry from the Guru Granth and from the Dasam Granth, the Book of the Tenth Guru, Gobind Singh, compiled some time after his death in 1708. Although the Guru Granth forms the centre of Sikh worship, the poetry of Guru Gobind Singh is highly esteemed by the Sikhs, and also forms part of their daily prayers.

The Guru Granth begins with the Jap, the most famous of the divinely-inspired poems, or bani, of Guru Nanak (1469-1539 CE), the founder of Sikhism. It is chanted daily by Sikhs and its first line, Ikk Oan Kar, literally "One Reality Is",[1] is the cornerstone of the faith. The Guru Granth and the Dasam Granth are an exposition of that One Reality, Its relation with our world, Its relation with each of us personally.

At the core of Guru Nanak's message is the understanding that all forms (saguna) are informed by the Formless (nirguna). Infinite and formless, the Ultimate Being is inherent within all forms and yet remains transcendent.

Whichever way we turn, we see our Source,
Says Nanak, the One has form, and yet the One is formless.[2]

You are the ocean and all are within You,
Without You, there is no other.[3]

You have a thousand eyes yet without eye are You,
You have a thousand faces yet without face are You,
You have a thousand feet yet without foot are You,
You have a thousand scents yet without scent are You,
...There is a Light in all, and that Light is You.[4]

We notice a marvellous dialectic of the particular and the universal, the physical and the metaphysical, the secular and the divine. "The Ultimate is in the individual, the individual is in

---

[1] Translated in *The Name of My Beloved* as: 'There is One Being".
[2] *The Name of My Beloved*, p. 225.
[3] Ibid., p. 130.
[4] Ibid., p. 150.

the Ultimate, / The two are one, there is no duality."[5] Western thinkers like Plato have tended to separate ideas and pure forms from everyday phenomena. In this view, only the universal and formless idea of the "rose" is real; the particular roses — those that can be seen, smelt and touched — are changeable, temporary, imperfect and, therefore, unreal. The Sikh perspective is to see the particular in the universal and the universal in the particular. A fluid connection is constantly maintained between them.

> You have one form, without compare,
> Here You are a beggar, there You are a king.[6]

The Gurus use an endless variety of images to evoke our connection with the Divine Reality: the potter with his clay, the blacksmith with his anvil, the mother nursing her child, the lady churning her pot of yogurt, the flowers in the garden, the animals of the earth. The entire world pulsates with divine potentiality, every atom vibrates with ultimate possibility. The Sikh understanding of Ultimate Reality is a dynamic and joyous experience.

Among the most beautiful ways by which the Gurus describe the special relationship between the Ultimate Reality and humanity is through the language of intimate human relationships. The words of Guru Arjan, "You are my father, You are my mother, You are my brother, You are my friend",[7] are regularly recited by the Sikhs. Images of conception, the growth of the unborn child in its mother's womb, and birth express the creative force of the Ultimate. "From mother's blood and father's semen, the human form is created," says

---

[5] Ibid., p. 236.

[6] Ibid., p. 134.

[7] Guru Granth, p. 103 (not included in this selection; reference is to the page in the original text)

the Guru Granth.[8] "In the warmth of the mother's womb are we first formed."[9]

Marriage, the highest experience of human love, is a particular form of this universal and formless love. It expresses the longing for Union with the Ultimate Reality. The Gurus often speak from the point of view of a woman, a bride awaiting her divine Groom, who addresses the Formless One as "Beloved".

> My mind and body yearn
>> but my Lover is far away in foreign lands.
> The Beloved does not come home, I am sighing to death,
>> and the lightning strikes fear in me.
> I lie alone on the bed, tormented;
>> mother, the pain is like death to me.
> Without the Divine One, how can there be sleep or hunger?
>> What clothing can soothe the skin?
> Nanak says, the bride is truly wed
>> when she is embraced by her Beloved.[10]

In giving these yearnings a female voice which speaks for all humanity, Sikh scripture opens out the definition of "man". The Sikh view is that a separation between male and female denies the wholeness of human nature. The Guru Granth emphasizes instead the significance of being human. In it, men and women share human suffering and hope. The explicit male and female imagery in the Guru Granth does not contradict the formless nature of the Ultimate One. Rather, it suggests a vast inclusiveness. The Ultimate Reality is above all and includes all. Whatever human beings can experience in their world is a part of the Metaphysical One.

---

[8] Ibid., p. 1002.

[9] Ibid., p. 156.

[10] *The Name of My Beloved*, p. 165.

As noted earlier, the starting point of the Guru Granth is this One Reality, expressed both orally and visually by Ikk Oan Kar. The visual symbol of this statement (see p. 49) begins with the numeral 1, recognizable to people of all languages and cultures. It is followed by the sign for Oan ("Reality", Sanskrit Aum) which embodies the notions of infinity and of the deepest reaches of the self, and is completed by the sign for Kar ("is"), an arch reaching away into space. This powerful and impeccably succinct symbol and statement, depicted on Sikh gateways, walls, medallions, canopies, fabric, and even jewellery, is followed by another equally precise revelation, Sat Naam, "Truth by Name". In the next stanza Guru Nanak explains further:

> Truth before time,
> Truth throughout time
> Truth here and now
> Says Nanak, Truth is evermore.

Immediately, he raises the question: "How then to be true? How then to break the wall of lies?" The transition from the True Name to true living is immediate and spontaneous. The Ultimate Reality is experiential. It is the stuff of life and It turns on the central Sikh concept of Naam, "Name". The Name is both the message and the messenger of Truth, the revelation and the revealer of Ultimate Reality. It is the Primal Guru, the Enlightener. It is what we can know of the Unknowable One Who pervades all existence and is beyond existence. This revelation and process of revelation is known as the "Name" of the Divine because it is analogous to when we learn the name of a person or thing and they thereby become known to us, are in some way revealed.

But the divine Name of Sikhism is no particular word or mantra; It is written within us and all around us.

There is no place without the Name.[11]

It is the revelation, inherent in the cosmos, presenting Itself to us in many ways.

For the destitute, Your Name is wealth,
For the homeless, Your Name is home,
For the lowly, Your Name is honour,
You grant Your gifts to every heart.[12]

As with the macrocosm, so too each individual body is a sacred space of the Name.

The ambrosial treasures of the divine Name
Rest within the body itself.'[13]

The One whose Name is Truth is present, vibrates and can be heard within our body. The individual self and the material body are affirmed and celebrated as houses of the Divine irrespective of gender, race, class and culture.

For the Sikh Gurus, Name is the only way of communing with the Divine: "Name is the highest action; Name is the highest duty."[14] To receive the Name is to experience the formless in this world of form, to know the transcendent within each and all.

Let us remember the Name and remind others as well,
By hearing, reciting and living the Name, we are liberated.
The Name is the essence, the form and the reality;

---

11 Ibid., p. 58.
12 Ibid., p. 194.
13 Guru Granth, p. 293.
14 Ibid., p. 353.

Says Nanak, let us praise the Name spontaneously.[15]

The Name is closely identified with the Word (Shabad) which also takes a central place in Sikh metaphysics. Creation, "written in a single stroke", is founded on the Word by which we may glean the Transcendent. Like the Name, the Word is intangible and insubstantial yet residing in the tangible and substantial. Like the Name, vibrations of the divine Word permeate us all, revealing the Ultimate within each of us. Everyone is endowed with anahad Shabad, the soundless Word.

But how can the Name be recognized within? How can the soundless Word deep inside be heard? Although the Name is no particular word, it is by words, especially those of the Guru Granth, that the Name is felt within. For Sikhs the Word is embodied in the Guru Granth and, like the strings of a sitar setting up resonance with the tambura, it can resonate the Word within our own body.

Guru Gobind Singh's Jaap in the Dasam Granth begins with the question of how to describe the One who has "no trait, no trace whatsoever . . . Who can recount all Your names? / The wise name You from Your actions"[16] he says, and then begins his Jaap, a hymn in speedy rhythm to exalt the Ultimate Reality using a plethora of words and compounds from Sanskrit, Persian and Arabic to name this Unnameable.

Unconquered / Unbreakable / Unchallenged / Unshakeable / Deep You are / Friend You are / Unencumbered / Utterly free / Enigmatic / Unknowable / Immortal / Unbound / Traceless / Placeless / Infinite / The Greatest / . . . Salutations to the Moon of moons / Salutations to the Sun of suns / Salutations to the

---

[15] *The Name of My Beloved*, p. 240.
[16] Ibid., p. 81.

Song of songs / Salutations to the Tune of tunes / Salutations
to the Dance of dances / Salutations to the Sound of sounds /
Salutations to the Hand of hands / Salutations to the Reason
of reason . . .[17]

Exalting the Ultimate Reality in beautiful poetry evokes a
harmonic response from a Truth that is already inside. In Sikh
worship, the Word embodied in the Guru Granth Sahib is not
just read or heard, it must echo blissfully within oneself. That
is why meditation and contemplation upon the Name is so
important. Melodious recitations and chanting of the scriptural
hymns which take place in gurudwaras and in homes are means
of entering into the deep recesses of our own selves. It is direct
and unmediated religious experience. There are no priests, no
commentators, no hierarchies between reciters/singer and
listeners, no social or gender obstacles between a person and
the sublime verses. In Name-adoration as this is known, the
mind and the senses, matter and spirit are together impelled
onwards in a holistic aesthetic experience. By reciting and
remembering the poems of the Guru Granth and Dasam Granth
with their ardent longing for the Divine, we unite with the
Beloved who is far away, the Beloved who is deep within. We
each find the Name of our Beloved.

The fact that the Guru Granth includes poetry of Hindu and
Islamic saints, and the divine names and concepts from these
faiths, demonstrates the Sikh attitude that the metaphysical
Reality is essentially common to people from all different faiths
and cultures. But while the Sikh Gurus respected the Hindu
and Islamic scriptures and mention them in a positive light,
they rejected the exclusive or final authority of any scripture.

---

[17] Ibid., pp. 86-8.

How many speak and begin to speak,
Many have spoken and gone,
And if their numbers were doubled again,
Still no one could say.
That One is as great as It chooses to be,
Nanak says, only the True One knows Itself.[18]

For the Gurus, religions converge beyond formalities and externals at the singular Truth. This is summed up in the Tenth Guru's statement:

. . . Hindus and Muslims are one.
The same Reality is the Creator and Preserver of all;
Know no distinctions between them.
The monastery and the mosque are the same;
So are the Hindu worship and the Muslim prayer.
Humans are all one![19]

According to Radhakrishnan, the renowned Hindu scholar and former President of India, Mahatma Gandhi was inspired by these words of Guru Gobind Singh in his moving public prayer,

Ishvara and Allah are Your names
Temples and mosques are Your home.[20]

Ethics

Sikh ethics are encapsulated in Guru Nanak's statement "Truth is higher than all, but higher still is true living."[21] All beings

[18] Ibid., p. 62.
[19] "Akal Ustat" by Guru Gobind Singb.
[20] S. Radhakrisnan, *The Principal Upanisads.* George Allen & Unwin Ltd, London, 1953, p. 139.
[21] Guru Granth, p. 62.

emerge from the singular Truth, so the Ultimate is within us all, But it is not sufficient simply to conceive the Truth; the Truth must be lived. Although there is no explicit statement about a hierarchy from plants to animals to humans, Sikhism suggests that humans are especially favoured in their capacity to approach the divine Reality. Sikh morality seeks the Eternal One, within our day-to-day existence. It is based on drawing the Ultimate Reality into the human situation.

What prevents the individual from uniting with the Ultimate? According to Sikhism, haumai, literally "I-myself", is the root cause of human suffering. It means investing oneself with pride and arrogance. By constantly centring on "I", "me" and "mine", the self is circumscribed as a particular person, away from the universal source. In his Jap, Guru Nanak provides the image of a wall: just as a wall creates barriers so does haumai. By building up the ego, the individual is divided from the One Reality. Duality comes into play. The ego sees itself in opposition to others, in opposition to the cosmos. The divine spark within remains obstructed. The singular harmony is broken. Such an existence is measured through competition, malice, ill-will towards others, and a craving for power. Blinded, the individual exists for himself or herself alone. The selfish person is called man mukh, "turned towards the ego", in contrast with one who remains in harmony with the divine Word and is called gur mukh, "turned towards the Guru". Dominated by haumai, a person never experiences the joy and infinity of the divine spark within. Haumai is a solid chain binding humans into the cycle of death and life.

The question then is, how can egotism be overcome? How can one be turned from selfishness to harmony with the Ultimate? Sikh ethical injunctions reiterate that pilgrimages, fasts and ascetic practices are of no avail. The walls of egotism can be shattered by following a simple formula found in Guru

Nanak's lap which contains three precepts: sunia, mania and manu kita bhau, respectively hearing, holding in mind (remembering) and loving.

Sunia literally signifies hearing, and in the Jap it means hearkening to the divine Word. It is the first step towards awakening to the transcendent Core of the universe. Hearing is the sense that most directly connects the conscious and the unconscious realms. According to Guru Nanak, by listening to the melodious Name, one fathoms the oceans of virtue. Stanzas 8 to 11 of the Jap (pp. 54—5) explain the vital role of listening. Through listening one accomplishes the faculties of all the gods, one gains knowledge of all the continents, one acquires the import of all the ancient texts, one learns all the techniques of meditation, one masters the expertise of all the sages of Hinduism and Islam (and by implication all religions) and through listening all suffering and distress is annulled. By hearing the divine Name the ultimate objective is achieved: one becomes immortal and is freed from the finitude of death. The refrain in these stanzas acknowledges that the devotees who hear the Name of the True One enjoy eternal bliss.

Although the Transcendent Reality is beyond all human terminology, words are important for they give us an inkling of the Formless One. Guru Nanak clearly maintains that the divine Names and the divine places are countless, and the countless worlds are inaccessible and unfathomable. Yet through words we name, through words we extol, through words we know, sing, and discuss. Through words all communication is conducted and expressed, and they are sanctioned by the Truth: "As the One utters, that is how the words are arranged." Hearing the divine Word constitutes the first step for Guru Nanak. Through sound we are initiated into an awareness of the Reality that permeates all space and time.

Mania means remembering the One, keeping the One

constantly in our mind. This process is not purely intellectual for it has connotations of trust and faith. It is the second step, for it is only after something is heard that it can enter the mind. According to Guru Nanak, this state is ineffable: who is to describe it? in what words? on what paper? with what pen? Remembering the divine Word is something that cannot be discussed or analysed. However, Guru Nanak also describes this state of faith in positive terms: through faith, the mind and intellect become more conscious. It is the pathway to liberation, wide open to everybody. According to the Gurus, those who believe in the divine Word are not only liberated from the constant bondage of birth and death but also assist in liberating their family and friends. Implicit here is the Sikh ethical structure, one in which self and society are integrally related. The individual is interconnected with the community, the Ultimate One links us all.

Manu kita bhau means to be full of love for the Divine. This state of devotion is the third step, one that goes beyond hearing the Name, and keeping the Name in mind. For those who attain this state, "Every thread of their being is drenched in love".[22] It is the highest form of action. Love is passionate and takes lovers to those depths of richness and fullness where there is freedom from all kinds of limitations of the self.

. . . the mind is enraptured by love,

Night and day it is in rapture, the self is lost.

If it please You, ego and greed are cast out.[23]

Cleansing through love and devotion is the starting point of Sikh ethics. Again and again in the Guru Granth, love is applauded as the supreme virtue:

---

[22] *The Name of My Beloved*, p. 191.

[23] Ibid., p. 168.

Pure, pure, utterly pure are they,
Says Nanak, who recite the Name with love.[24]

As noted earlier, through the symbol of the bride, Sikh scripture explores the power of intimacy and passion in the human relationship with the Divine. Through the bride who is for ever seeking union with her Groom, the Gurus express the ardent love and longing for the Ultimate Reality.

Embraced by her Beloved,
   the woman savours all delights.
Only she who pleases her Lover is embraced,
   and she alone is the true bride.
She makes her body with its nine doors the lofty palace,
   her own house enshrines the Beloved.
I am all Yours and You are mine, my Dearest,
   I revel in Your love night and day.[25]

Love is the only path to ultimate liberation:

I tell the truth, do listen to me,
they alone who love, find the Beloved.[26]

The passion for the singular Creator is manifested in acts of love towards all fellow beings. The institutions of langar (community meal), seva (deeds of love and service), sangat (congregation) and the khalsa (fellowship founded by Guru Gobind Singh) are a means of providing a practical outlet for this disposition of love. Since all are equally the progeny of the

---

[24] Ibid., p. 221.
[25] Ibid., p. 162.
[26] Ibid., p. 119.

Infinite One, they have to be treated as kinsfolk. The response of love is vital to Sikh metaphysics and ethics alike.

Mysticism and Cosmology

The mystical experience in Sikhism is not apart or separate from the everyday; rather, the deeper the awareness of the Transcendent, the more vibrant is the participation in the secular world. In the final lines of the Jap, Guru Nanak presents five stages by which human beings can journey into the Ultimate Reality. They are the realms, or regions, of duty, knowledge, beauty, grace and truth.

Dharam Khand is the Region of Duty or Dharam (similar to the Sanskrit ideal of Dharma) here on earth where we are all active agents. Here we human beings should co-exist harmoniously and ethically with all beings. Time is a major factor at this level of existence. It is described as a region made up of nights and seasons and dates and days. All the elements — air, water, fire and earth — and all the compounds produced from them are a part of this physical universe with the earth as the axis, uniting all species. "In it are colourful beings and lifestyles, / Infinite are their names and infinite their forms"[27] Guru Nanak tells us. Although there are innumerable varieties of species, all are interconnected, and there is no implication of any disjunctions or divisions of gender, race, and class in this organic Earth. We are all provided with the opportunity to act ethically and purposefully. Earthly existence is not to be shunned but to be lived fully and intensely. Actions are important, for whatever we do has an effect: as we sow, so do we reap. The sense of morality is developed in this region.

Gyan Khand, the second stage, is the Region of Knowledge. Here the mind expands. The individual becomes cognizant of

---

[27] Ibid., p. 65.

the vastness of creation, which is expressed in many different ways. In this region there are innumerable varieties of atmospheres, water and fire. It is made up of millions of inhabited planets like our earth, countless mountains, countless moons, suns and constellations. This sphere also contains innumerable gods and goddesses. In contrast with the vastness of infinite space, the smallness of the self is experienced. Knowledge of the widening horizons makes one stand fully in awe of the Invisible Creator. But knowledge here is not abstract. It does not pertain to ideas nor is it an accumulation of facts about the varied planets. Rather, it is the experience of dissolution of the ego. The selfish manipulation of others gives way to an all-embracing feeling. Limitations and prejudices are destroyed, creating an all-accepting and welcoming attitude.

Saram Khand, the third stage, is the Realm of Beauty where the human faculties and sensibilities are sharpened and refined. It is a magnificent region, one whose beauty cannot be adequately described. Here the aesthetic sensitivity, an important stage in the mystical voyage, is developed. As Guru Nanak explains, "one who can appreciate fragrance will alone know the flower".[28] By refining our physical senses, we appreciate the marvellous presence of the Metaphysical Reality everywhere in our world. We begin to know that Reality Itself. Again the Sikh worldview does not distinguish between physical, mental or spiritual sensibilities. Together they constitute the person and together they are developed in this realm of beauty and art. In Guru Nanak's words, "Here consciousness, wisdom, mind and discernment are honed."[29] The cultivation of the aesthetic faculties opens the way to the next stage.

Karam Khand, the fourth stage, is the Realm of Grace. It is described as the abode of those who cherish none other than

[28] Guru Granth, p. 725.
[29] *The Name of My Beloved*, p. 66.

the Transcendent One. "Here heroes and mighty warriors dwell."[30] Who are these warriors and heroes? The true hero, says Nanak, is one who kills the evil of egotism within. Real might and strength lie in overcoming the ego. Herculean muscle and power is not the ideal. In Sikh thought, "Conquering ourselves, we conquer the world".[31] Conquest of nations and peoples is much easier than the conquest of the self. Heroines and heroes residing in this region are in full control of themselves and they are exempt from the cycle of birth and death. "They know bliss, for the True One is imprinted on their minds."[32] Firm in their conviction and full of joy, they blithely enter the final stage.

Sach Khand, the Realm of Truth, is the fifth and final stage. The Metaphysical One is named "Truth". The Realm of Truth is therefore the sphere of the Timeless One, the abode of the Formless Reality. As we enter into it, we are in the home of Ultimate Reality, we are at home with Ultimate Reality: there is a total union between the human and the Divine. The loving gaze of the Divine upon the seekers and their joyful vision of that One come together in this realm.

But this stage is hard to describe: "as hard as iron"[33] is the simile employed by Guru Nanak. "Here are continents, constellations and universes / Whose limits cannot be told."[34] The individual thus comes face to face with Infinity. The focus here turns from the individual to the Transcendent. The individual partakes of the qualities of the True One. The finite individual becomes free from the cycle of migrations and transmigrations. As the microcosmic self is emancipated from the limitations of space, time, gender and causality, there is the

---

[30] Ibid.
[31] Ibid., p. 63.
[32] Ibid., p. 67.
[33] Ibid.
[34] Ibid.

experience of utter joy. The Sikh mystical journey is not a journey away from our world. Rather, it is grounded in and of this earth. It is here in our everyday existence that we develop our moral, intellectual, aesthetic and spiritual capacities and experience the Ultimate Reality. The journey begins and ends in love for fellow beings, an immersion into our particular and material and secular world, and an insight into beauty and intimate relationships here and now. Since the transcendent goal does not lie high above, we need not climb up anywhere. With its maps and charts drafted totally on the longitudes and latitudes of our planet earth, Sikh mysticism is based on drawing the Ultimate Reality into the human situation. Thus we live in the truest sense, living as life would be in Sach Khand, the Realm of Truth.

From Guru Nanak to the Guru Granth

Nanak, who lived in the culturally diverse Punjab of the fifteenth century, disappeared for three days while bathing in a river and was thought to have drowned. On the third day he reappeared. He had been in communion with the Supreme Being.

It is said that for a whole day after his emergence from the river Bein, Guru Nanak sat silently in deep meditation. "There is no Hindu, there is no Muslim" are the first words he spoke. This statement should not be misinterpreted; Guru Nanak was not making a value judgment about, nor refuting, the religious life of the Hindus and Muslims of his day. He was pointing to the oneness of the Transcendent that translates into the oneness and equality of humanity. Nor did Guru Nanak's statement propose religious uniformity. He was not asking people to abandon their faith and adopt another, but stressing the fundamental, common truth underlying the diverse faiths and systems of belief. His insight was to become the philosophical and ethical foundation for his Sikhs, his "followers."

This was a simple announcement, and yet a significant one in the context of India of his day. To a society torn by conflict, he brought a vision of common humanity — a vision which transcended all barriers of creed and caste, race and country.[1]

Guru Nanak was born on 15 April 1469 in Talwandi, a small Indian village (in present day Pakistan). His father, Kalyan Chand

---

[1] Harbans Singh, *Berkeley Lectures on Sikhism*. Guru Nanak Foundation, New Delhi, 1983.

of the Bedi clan of Khatris, was the village accountant for the local Muslim landlord. His mother, Tripta, was well known as a pious and gentle lady. Nanak was named after his older sister Nanaki. From an early age, Nanak was opposed to rituals and to the caste system. Inclined towards the life of the spirit, he lost interest in the rigid discipline of formal schooling. His father, no doubt upset, sent Nanak to graze cattle. Soon the village of Talwandi was buzzing with miraculous accounts of Nanak the herdsman which are recorded in the Janamsakhis, the accounts of his birth and life,[2] and which include a description of his revelation at the age of twenty-eight while bathing in the Bein:

> As the Primal Being willed, Nanak the devotee was ushered into the Divine Presence. Then a cup filled with amrit (nectar) was given him with the command, "Nanak, this is the cup of Name-adoration (naam piala). Drink it . . . I am with you and I do bless and exalt you. Whoever remembers you will have my favour. Go, rejoice, in My Name and teach others to do so . . . I have bestowed upon you the gift of My Name. Let this be your calling." Nanak offered his salutations and stood up.[3]

The genesis of the Sikh religion is traced to this epiphany in which Nanak had profound insight into the existence as well as into the nature of the Transcendent. He received "the cup of Name", that is, he heard the divine Command, held the cup, savoured its ambrosial contents, and recognized the absolute Truth. To drink the ambrosia of the Name is to imbibe the

---

[2] In the sixteenth century, some time after Guru Nanak's death, his followers wrote short accounts of his birth and life. These narratives are the first prose works in the Punjabi language of Guru Nanak's region of India, the Punjab. They are called Janamsakhis from the Punjabi words janam, "birth", and sakhi, "story".

[3] Bhai Vir Singh, ed., *Puratan Janamsakhi*. Khalsa Samachar, Amritsar, 1948, pp. 16-17.

sapiential quality of knowledge received from the Divine. Guru Nanak's experience was at once sensuous and metaphysical. (For a further discussion of the "Name" see pp. 4-9.)

The vision of the Ultimate Oneness marked the beginning of Guru Nanak's mission. He was charged to deliver the message bequeathed to him through the vision, a message which essentially entails discerning and rejoicing in the infinite and singular reality beyond the fragmented parts and particles. Guru Nanak celebrated the favour of receiving the Name through a song of praise; and song was to be the medium of his divine inspiration ever after.

All of Guru Nanak's teaching is set forth in verse. His genius was best expressed in the poetical attitude. No other way would have been adequate to the range and depth of his mood — his fervent longing for the Infinite, his joy and wonder at the beauty and vastness of His creation, his tender love for his fellowmen, his moral speculation and his concern at the suppression and exaction to which the people in his day were subject. His compositions reveal an abounding imagination and a subtle aesthetic sensitivity.[4]

Whatever he said, and however he said it, Nanak acknowledged that it was divinely inspired. "As the Word comes to me, that is how I deliver it."[5] This poetic mode was to be the starting point of the Sikh scripture, the Guru Granth.

For twenty-four years after his revelation, Guru Nanak travelled throughout India and beyond spreading the divine Word. He was accompanied during most of his travels by his Muslim

---

[4] Harbans Singh, *Guru Nanak and Origins of the Sikh Faith*. Publication Bureau, Punjabi University, Patiala, 1994, pp. 215-16.

[5] Guru Granth, p. 722.

companion, Mardana, who played on the rebec while Guru Nanak sang songs of intense love for the Divine One. The dress he wore as he set out on his journeys combined elements of Hindu and Muslim wear, a mixture which was symbolic of his common message for all peoples. Recognizing and accepting the religious plurality in which he lived, he freely mixed with the exponents of different traditions. Throughout his life, he continued to preach for a common humanity which, to his way of thinking, transcended all racial, social, religious and gender barriers and which he wished people of all faiths to perceive and cherish. During his extensive travels throughout India, he visited places of worship belonging to various religious traditions — Hindu temples, Muslim mosques, Buddhist viharas, and Sufi khanaqahs — and attended their fairs and festivals. In the Guru Granth we come across evidence that he met with yogis, Sufis, and naths. When he met Muslims, he adjured them to be faithful to the teaching of their faith; when he met Hindus, he urged them to abide by the tenets of their own tradition. The essential and eternal truth which lay beyond all externals and particularisms was the core of Guru Nanak's vision of the Transcendent One.

The rich but simple style of his teaching drew people from different religious, cultural and social backgrounds. Wherever Guru Nanak went, people began to follow him, calling themselves Sikhs, a Punjabi word which means "disciple". It can be traced to the Sanskrit shishya and the Pali sekka. Bhai Gurdas (1551-1636), the first Sikh historian and theologian, viewed this new faith as "a needle which sews materials that are ripped asunder, bringing harmony to the torn and conflicting groups".[6]

At the end of his travels, Guru Nanak settled in Kartarpur, a Punjabi village he had founded on the right bank of the river Ravi. A community of disciples grew around him here. It was

---

6 Bhai Vir Singh, *Varan Bhai Gurdas*. Khalsa Samacar. Amritsar, 1977, var. 33.4.

not a monastic order of any kind, but a fellowship of men and women engaged in the ordinary occupations of life. Guru Nanak established two important Sikh institutions: those of sangat and langar. Sangat is the holy congregation where men and women sit together to recite praises of the Divine; langar is the community refectory where men and women, irrespective of caste and creed, eat a common meal. Both have been potent factors in fostering the values of equality, fellowship and humility, and in affirming a new and dynamic sense of "family".

A further crucial development was the appointment of a successor. Before he passed away in 1539, Guru Nanak announced that his disciple Lahina was henceforth to be named "Angad", literally "part of his own body". This phenomenon is described in the Guru Granth as the transference of Light: "And now the writ of Angad ran instead of Nanak's; for, the Light was the same, the Way the same, only the body had changed."[7] Bhai Gurdas depicts it as one flame lighting another. For the Sikhs this process was repeated successively until the Tenth Guru, Gobind Singh, ended the line of personal Guruship and made the Granth the Guru eternal. We learn from Bhai Gurdas that Guru Nanak carried a manuscript of his poetry under his arm,[8] perhaps foreseeing the need for a scripture for the growing Sikh community. When Angad succeeded Guru Nanak, he inherited this record and also composed metaphysical poetry of his own. For him, the divine Word had an aesthetic as well as an epistemological value: "It is ambrosia, it is the essence of all, it emerges from deep knowledge and intense concentration."[9] Thus, while heightening and refining the senses, poetry also reveals the essence of existence itself. Guru Angad added his

---

[7] Guru Granth, p. 966.

[8] Bhai Vir Singh op. cit., var. 1.32.

[9] Guru Granth, p. 1243.

poetry to that of Guru Nanak's collection, and signed it too with the name "Nanak". It was Guru Angad who developed the Gurmukhi script in which the Guru Granth was to be written.

As the succession of Guruship passed on, so did the verse of one Guru to the next. Each valued and nurtured the literary inheritance from his predecessor and, adding his own compositions also under the pseudonym "Nanak", he would pass on the poetic legacy to the next. Guru Nanak was cherished as the founder of something new and different, and they felt that they were simply continuing his message.

The Compilation of the Guru Granth

In 1603, Guru Arjan, the Fifth Guru, took upon himself the compilation of the Granth. Guru Arjan had two reasons for taking up this physically and intellectually demanding task. First, he realized that the community needed a text that would encapsulate the Sikh worldview — a Granth (book) for the Panth (community). The fellowship of Sikhs had increased and spread, calling for a common message for its spiritual and moral life. Guru Arjan himself had travelled widely. There had been a famine in the Punjab, so the Guru travelled from village to village, helping people sink wells and undertake other works of public welfare. As a consequence many more people were drawn into the Sikh fold. There was thus an urgency for the revelation coming from Guru Nanak and his successors to be crystallized. Second, there was the problem of "counterfeit" works. Guru Ram Das, the Fourth Guru, had bypassed his older sons and appointed Arjan to the Guruship, causing a rift with Pirthi Chand, his eldest son. Pirthi and his gifted son Meharban began to compose sacred poetry under the name of Nanak. To fix the seal on the sacred Word and to preserve it for posterity Guru Arjan began to codify the Sikh literary legacy into an authorized volume.

Bhai Gurdas was called upon for help. He and Guru Arjan retreated to a serene and picturesque spot in the thick of a forest outside Amritsar and started work. Today, this site in the southern part of the city is marked by a shrine called Ramsar. There was a vast amount of poetic material; selections had to be made from the works of all the preceding four Gurus, as well as Guru Arjan's own superb and extensive body of poetry. Furthermore, whatever was in harmony with the Sikh Gurus, even the sayings of the Hindu or Muslim saints, was also to be included. Finally, what was genuinely composed by the Gurus had to be sifted from what was incorrectly attributed to them. With literary finesse and scholarly precision, Guru Arjan acted as compiler and editor while Bhai Gurdas was the amanuensis using the Gurmukhi script of Punjabi.

The organisation of the poetry was musical. Apart from a few hymns, the entire collection is organized into thirty-one sections, each section containing poems in one melodic scale (rag). These rags appear in the following order: Sri, Majh, Gauri, Asa, Gujri, Devgandhari, Bihagara, Vadahans, Sorath, Dhanasri, Jaitsri, Todi, Bairari, Tilang, Suhi, Bilaval, Gaund, Ramkali, Nut-Narayan, Mali Gaura, Maru, Tukhari, Kedara, Bhairo, Basant, Sarang, Malar, Kanra, Kalyan, Prabhat and Jaijawanti. Each measure has its particular characteristic, its timing and season. For instance, the first, Sri, meaning "supreme", is one of the parent measures from which the others are derived. It is compared to the philosopher's stone, supreme among other stones, which transforms baser metals into gold. It is sung in the evening, when darkness takes over. In content too, it expresses the darkness of ignorance and superstition in which Guru Nanak's society was enfolded. Seasonally, the measure Sri is associated with extreme heat and cold, indicating an intensity of emotion. The poets in this measure are heard expressing their ardent yearning for the Divine.

Within each of these thirty-one sections, the poetry of the Gurus was organised in the order of their succession. We know that all the Gurus signed their compositions with the name of Nanak to show that they were continuing his work. This was a little confusing, of course, so at the top of each work Guru Arjan wrote Mahalla 1 if the poem was written by the First Guru, Mahalla 2 if it was written by the Second Guru, and so on. Mahalla means "body," and it indicates that the Gurus are different bodies of the one spirit of Nanak which they all share. So a poem by a particular Guru will be titled first by the name of the rag to which it is sung (this may or may not include the word "rag"), then by the mahalla number. There may also be an actual title to the poetry as for example with Sodar Rag Asa Mahalla 1. Sodar means "Gate" and is the title, Asa is the rag, and Mahalla 1 indicates it is the composition of Guru Nanak.

These poems by the first five Gurus were followed by those of numerous Hindu and Muslim saints. (For a list of the contributors, see Appendix Two, p. 248).

The completion of the Granth was an occasion of great celebration. Later Sikh history compares the festivities with those of a wedding. Huge quantities of karahprashad, the Sikh sacred food (made up of sugar, butter, water and flour), were distributed. Sikhs travelled for miles to witness the colourful procession that would bear the sacred volume to Harimandir, the temple at Amritsar, a special place for Sikh worship, which was the inspiration of Amar Das, the Third Guru. Work on the Harimandir had begun under Ram Das, the Fourth Guru, in 1577. A structure of great architectural beauty, the shrine was completed in Guru Arjan's period, in 1601, only three years before the completion of the Guru Granth. The Harimandir came to be known as the Golden Temple after the Sikh Maharajah Ranjit Singh had it reconstructed and plated with gold. On 16 August 1604 the Guru Granth was ceremoniously installed in the inner sanctuary of the Harimandir. Bhai Buddha, the surviving elderly and venerable Sikh devotee of Guru Nanak, actually carried it on his head while Guru Arjan walked behind holding the whisk over it in homage. Musicians played hymns from the sacred text. Bhai Buddha opened the Granth with reverence to obtain the divine command (hukam) from it; Guru Arjan stood in attendance behind. At dusk, the Granth was taken to a specially built chamber. There it was placed on a pedestal while Guru Arjan slept on the floor by its side. Such was the veneration shown to the Granth by the Gurus themselves. The original copy of the sacred book is preserved to this day at Kartarpur, a town near Jalandhar founded by Guru Arjan.

The Founding of the Khalsa and the Apotheosis of the Guru Granth

By Guru Arjan's time, therefore, the Sikhs had received both a sacred space and a sacred text. These were both important in moulding Sikh self-consciousness. The Harimandir provided a central place for gathering and worship. The Granth gave the Sikh message a concrete form. It not only became their spiritual and religious guide but also shaped their intellectual and cultural environment. These were significant events in the crystallization of the Sikh faith.

As the Sikh faith began to solidify and the Sikhs grew in number, the Muslim rulers of India became concerned. Guru Arjan was imprisoned by the governor of the Punjab. In 1606 he was executed. The martyrdom of the Fifth Guru generated a strong impulse of resistance and inaugurated a new era of militarism. Instead of the rosary and other saintly emblems, his son Guru Hargobind, the Sixth Guru, wore a warrior's equipment for the ceremonies of succession. He put on two swords: one was declared the symbol of his spiritual (piri) and the other of his temporal (miri) investiture, emphasizing how in the Sikh faith the worldly and the other-worldly are not separate.[10]

This act of combining miri and piri in two swords marked an important development in the evolution of the Sikh community — the development of a martial spirit. Since peaceful resistance to oppression had proved abortive, the Guru recognized recourse to the sword as a lawful alternative. He raised a small armed band of Sikhs and sent out messages that disciples in the future should come with gifts of horses and weapons. In 1609, to defend the town of Amritsar, he built a fortress called the Iron Fort. Another symbol of temporal authority instituted by Guru Hargobind was the Akal Takht (the Throne of the Timeless One) in front of the Harimandir. The Harimandir was for prayer, the Akal Takht for the conduct of the community's secular affairs.

But it was the martyrdom of Guru Tegh Bahadur (the Ninth Guru) in Delhi that finally consolidated the martial aspect of Sikhism. This Sikh Guru challenged the policy of the Muslim rulers of converting Hindus by force, and for this defence of religious freedom he was executed in 1675. His son and successor, Guru Gobind Singh, the Tenth Guru, though only nine years of age then, provided vigorous leadership to the Sikhs. His first task was to infuse a new spirit among his people.

Guru Gobind Singh fulfilled his aspiration for religious freedom in 1699 by inaugurating the Khalsa, the Order of the Pure. It was a casteless and self-abnegating body of Sikhs ready to take up arms to fight against oppression. The day was Vaisakhi, New Year's Day in the north Indian calendar. The town was Anandpur in the Shivalik hills. Chanting verses from the Guru Granth, Guru Gobind Singh began the new initiation into the Khalsa by churning water, poured into a steel bowl, with a

---

[10] Harbans Singh, *Guru Tegh Bahadur*. Sterling, New Delhi, 1982, p. 17.

double-edged sword. His wife, Mata Sahib Kaur, came forward and dropped sugar crystals into the vessel. Sweetness through the feminine hand was thus mingled with the alchemy of iron.

The occasion marked a dramatic departure from the past. The five to whom the rites of initiation were administered by Guru Gobind Singh were given the surname of Singh, meaning "lion", and were ever after to wear the emblems of the Khalsa, popularly known as the Five Ks. These were kesha or uncut hair; kangha, a comb tucked into the kesha to keep it tidy in contrast with the recluses who kept it matted as a token of their having renounced the world; kara, a steel bracelet symbolizing strength and unity; kachha, short breeches worn by the soldiers of that time; and kirpan, a sword. Their rebirth into the new order represented the annihilation of their family (caste) lineage, of their confinement to a hereditary occupation, of all their earlier beliefs and creeds, and of the rituals they had so far observed. They were enjoined to help the weak and fight the oppressor. Guru Gobind Singh reiterated the First Sikh Guru's message to have faith in the One, and consider all human beings equal, irrespective of caste and religion. In Guru Gobind Singh's words:

I wish you all to embrace one creed and follow one path, rising above all differences of religion as now practised. Let the four Hindu castes, who have different duties laid down for them in their scriptures, abandon them altogether, and adopting the way of mutual help and co-operation, mix freely with one another. Do not follow the old scriptures. Let none pay homage to the Ganges and other places of pilgrimage which are considered to be holy in the Hindu religion, or worship the Hindu deities such as Rama, Krishna, Brahma and Durga, but all should cherish faith in the teachings of Guru Nanak and his successors. Let each of the four castes receive my Baptism of the double-edged sword, eat out of the same vessel, and feel no aloofness from, or contempt for one another.[11]

Guru Nanak's vision to affirm and celebrate the oneness of Ultimate Reality and the oneness of humanity was given a practical form by Guru Gobind Singh. His verse "recognize the single caste of humanity" is very popular in modern times and is recited by Sikhs in India and abroad. The initiation through steel was open to both men and women. Women were also to wear the five emblems of the Khalsa. As men received the surname Singh, women received the surname Kaur, signifying "princess", and they retained this name whether single or married. Thus the patriarchal structure of society was modified. Men and women no longer traced their lineage or occupation to the "father"; as "Singh" and "Kaur" both became equal partners in the new family of Sikhism.

Shortly before he passed away, Guru Gobind Singh made a momentous decision. On 6 October, 1708, he asked his disciples to bring the Granth to him. In a manner reminiscent of Guru Nanak's appointment of Angad as his successor, Guru Gobind Singh placed a five paise coin and a coconut before the Granth and bowed his head in veneration before it. He told the gathered community that it was his commandment that henceforth they acknowledge the Granth in his place. The Granth was thus apotheosized as the Guru. Personal guruship came to an end. Succession now passed to the Guru Granth in perpetuity. Sikhs were not to perceive Guru in any other form. The Word alone was to be the Guru Eternal. From that day on, the Sikhs in their daily supplications, morning and evening, recite: "Acknowledge the Guru Granth as the visible body of the

---

[11] Sujan Rai Bhandari Batalia, *Khulasat-ut-Tawarikh*. Quoted in Kapur Singh, *The Baisakhi of Guru Gobind Singh*. Hind Publishers, Jullundur, 1959, pp. 4-5.

Gurus." The Guru Granth is thus revered as both the physical body of the Gurus and the metaphysical corpus of their poetry.

The Guru Granth in Daily Life

The Guru Granth has been the continuing spiritual and historical authority for Sikhs as well as a primary source for their literary inspiration. Through their scripture, Sikhs have been able to observe their faith more fully and more vividly. The community's ideals, institutions and rituals have derived their meaning from the Guru Granth. In the words of the eminent Sikh scholar Harbans Singh, "the physical presence of the Guru Granth and its sublime poetry have constituted the twin regulative principles for the psyche of the Sikhs and their conduct".[12]

The shrine which houses the Guru Granth is called a gurudwara, literally, a door (dwara) to ultimate enlightenment (guru'). But many Sikhs keep the holy volume in their homes, paying full respect by keeping it in a separate room, on a pedestal, draped in silks. Whether in homes or in gurudwaras, the holy book is ceremoniously opened in the morning and closed in the evening. It is also present at special gatherings such as weddings, name-giving ceremonies, birthdays, commemorations and house-blessing events. In such functions, it is carried onto the lawns or verandahs or drawing-rooms and paid the utmost homage. Wherever the Book is kept or heard, that space is revered by the Sikhs. A line in the Guru Granth says that paradise is where the holy verses are recited. As we noted, the Word embodied in the Guru Granth is present and resonates within our own bodies.

The Guru Granth is set at the very centre of the gurudwaras. These vary in scale, for a gurudwara in a tiny village can be

---

[12] Harbans Singh, *Sri Guru Grauth Sahib: Guru Eternal for the Sikhs*. Academy of Sikh Religion and Culture, Patiala, 1988, p. 19.

small, and they vary in style, for a gurudwara in India could be different from one in America. But even from a distance any gurudwara can be identified by the yellow triangular flag, flying overhead and carrying the emblem of the Sikh Khalsa (nishan sahib). The emblem of the Khalsa is an upright double-edged sword set in a circle, which in turn is encircled by a curved sword on either side.[13] This also appears on the walls, windows and doors of the gurudwara.

The traditional gurudwaras can also be recognized by their white domes and minarets leading the eyes towards the infinite skies. They have a large courtyard which provides an immediate feeling of expansiveness. There is a pool within this and the combination of the transparent waters extending horizontally and the diaphanous designs in marble going vertically creates a calm and holistic effect. A walkway goes around the pool, and devotees are seen bathing in the water, sitting on the edge saying prayers, and circumambulating in a contemplative mood. Gurudwaras have four doors, an architectural statement that they welcome people from the four castes. There is no womblike chamber or altar to which only the chosen are admitted. There are no sculptures or images incarnating deity in any form. The congregation can gather inside or outside, it does not really matter. There are no chairs and the entire congregation sits on large mats spread on the floors. The centre, of course, is the Guru Granth. With its metaphysical poetry in sensuous imagery leading the self to the Ultimate Reality beyond, it is readily present to all people from the four directions.

Just as the words of the Guru Granth are not static, in the same way the geometric designs on the gurudwara floors and the floral designs on its walls of marble and stone are not closures either. Abstraction, symmetry, rhythm and repetition are

---

[13] See pp. 27-30 for the Khalsa and the significance of this emblem.

essential characteristics of Sikh architecture. Abstract patterns make possible a passage into another world beyond the senses. Symmetric designs serenely emerging from a multiplicity of intricate details create a surging sentiment of tranquillity. The black and white marble slabs upon which the devotees walk are repeated rhythmically. So are the stylized flowers and birds and arabesques and lattice-work on the walls and sides. The structure itself repeats its arches and domes, pillars and kiosks, windows and storeys. Amongst the unending repetitions that one walks upon, touches on the sides, sees on the building, the melodious Word is heard. The rhythmic repetitions create a dynamic movement for the senses and imagination. Together they are impelled onwards. Any feeling of uneasiness gives way to harmony; doubts and dualities begin to dissolve; the ignorant psyche is inspired to discover its essential spark. Through its finite structures the gurudwara creates an energetic movement towards the infinite Transcendent.

Whether publicly in the gurudwaras or privately at home, Sikhs bow in front of their Book with their heads covered and shoes removed. They stand in front of it in homage, or sit on the floor while the Guru Granth is always placed on a higher platform. Amidst joyous recitations, the Guru Granth is opened at dawn. This opening ceremony is called prakash karna, literally "making the light manifest". Any Sikh may perform prakash; in Sikh homes, the duty often rotates among family members, and, in gurudwaras, among the congregation. The Book is draped in rich silks and brocades. It is placed on quilted mats, and supported by three cushions, one under each side and one in the centre. A canopy hangs over it for protection, and a whisk is waved over it as a sign of respect. Those present stand humbly in front of it and recite Ardas, a prayer of supplication.[14] The

14 See pp. 141-5.

Guru Granth is then opened at random, and the passage at the top of the left-hand page is read aloud. This passage is called vak or hukam, the message or order for the day.

After dusk, the Guru Granth is closed. The closing ritual is called sukhasan, which means "to sit comfortably". Again, Ardas is said and vak taken. With recitations of evening prayers, the book is ceremoniously closed.

From East to West

The project to create this book has been an exciting one. Trying to translate the sacred songs from the Guru Granth and the Dasam Granth, I felt like the Chinese jar described by T. S. Eliot: "still / Moves perpetually in its stillness". All these months, I was sitting in Ireland working quietly on my translations, but I was moving very quickly between different zones: past and future, East and West, sacred and secular.

I was nurtured on the original poetry. Every morning I heard the Japji and Shabad Hazare melodiously recited by my mother; every evening I heard Rahiras and Kirtan Sohila from my father who held me in his arms and strolled on the terrace in our home in the Punjab. Often I would visit the gurudwara with my grandmother. As a part of the congregation, we would hear the verses sung, we would hear them read, and we would hear them interpreted. We would also join the congregation in the singing of the hymns. All these moments were full of awe, marked by something numinous and wonderful. I may not have understood the meaning of the verses but they became a part of my being and continued to resonate somewhere deep inside.

Now to translate those verses for a publication in the English language! I sit at a computer. I am surrounded by texts, dictionaries, translations, commentaries. Behind me are my editors and publishers; in front, my readers. The whole scenario is different. At home in the Punjab, the very language of the Sikh verse is given the greatest respect. In our house, even Punjabi newspapers in the Gurmukhi script were not allowed to be put on the ground. Any volume containing the sacred poetry is deeply honoured. When I studied the texts with our

Gyaniji (scriptural scholar) over my summer holidays from America, I was reprimanded for having tea during our sessions or for not rinsing my mouth before I resumed after a tea-break. Now miles away in Ireland, should I cover my head as I pick up the texts? Should I be listening to popular music while I work? Should I even have a cup of tea as I hold and read through the sacred poetry? The process of translation has been more than a conversion of a text from one language into another: it has been moving back and forth between the sacred and the academic worlds. Undoubtedly, the process has been elating; it has been daunting.

There has been the sheer joy of returning to my poetry, to my past. For, first of all, the process of translation requires a sound understanding of the original. The meaning and rich philosophical import of the poetry that was heard and read earlier in life had to be fully recovered. The intimacy between the sound of the verses I had heard from my mother's lips and their sense that I was now discovering with my own one-year-old daughter pottering around was a wonderful experience. Time acquired a timeless quality.

The project has enabled me to renew old friendships and make new ones. To work with my old family friends Dr Narinder S. Kapany and Dr W. Owen Cole has been a memorable experience. I am especially delighted to have found a close associate in Kerry Brown, the editor of ISLT. Her sincere appreciation of the Gurus' poetry was most inspiring. Her excitement carried over the Irish Sea and spurred me on. I am truly grateful to her for her attraction to the simplicity of Sikh poetry, and her constant support for maintaining the freshness of the Gurus' Word in the English language.

These translations also afford me an opportunity to share my heritage with my students and academic colleagues in the West. The rich literature of the Sikhs still remains inaccessible, as

Sikhism is one of the traditions that is still relatively unexplored. During my course of study and teaching in the United States, I found that Sikhism simply does not seem to be a part of world religion courses. Even professors who would like to include it find themselves with a practical problem: "What primary text do we use?" During conferences and seminars like the National Endowment for the Humanities, my colleagues have pressed hard on this issue. Teaching Religious Studies in a New England Liberal Arts College for almost a decade, I myself have felt a real need for a basic book in the area of Sikh literature. Of course no translation can replace the original text, but how to introduce this Asian text in a Western classroom? An accessible translation is urgently needed. Several translations of the entire corpus exist but they are unwieldy. The standard four-volumed sets published in India are not only difficult to get hold of but also difficult to hold.

Furthermore, the translations that exist are archaic. During my seminars and classes I am amazed at the way in which translators and exegetes in the English language have managed to make the rich and inclusive literature of the Sikhs so "foreign" and "alien", one which can only be approached with distance and detachment. This has been a problem with translations from India for a long time. Yeats correctly identified it when he commented that the works of eminent scholars are strewn with latinized and hyphenated words: "polyglot phrases, sedentary distortions of unnatural English muddles, muddied by 'Lo! Verily', and 'Forsooth'".[1] Yeats was talking about the Upanishads when he made this remark. Things may have improved in major Hindu texts, but unfortunately there still hasn't been much change in translations of Sikh literature.

---

[1] W.B. Yeats and Shree Purohit Swami, *The Ten Principal Upanishads*. Macmillan, New York, 1937, reissued 1975, pp. 7-8.

I also find the existing translations androcentric. The Ultimate Reality of the Sikhs is beyond gender and yet invariably this metaphysical Being is translated into a male deity. I hope, in particular, my translations will reach out to women. The feminine imagery in Sikh poetry presents a plurality of viewpoints and provides a host of options for self-discovery. As we launch into the twenty-first century, the Sikh message of love and the equality of men and women can offer a new meaning and a new authenticity to our goal of cultural and sexual equality.

Sadly, the meaning of their sacred verse remains closed even for many Sikhs. The vocabulary of the Guru Granth, which includes Sanskrit, Arabic and Persian terms, poses problems for an average Punjabi. Decoding the poetry of Guru Gobind Singh, laced as it is with highly subtle and ornate metaphors and imagery, and replete with mythological allusions and linguistic innovations, is an even harder task. Furthermore, the British legacy induces young Punjabi Sikhs to study English and Western philosophies and literatures, drawing them away from their own mother-tongue and their own literary heritage. Taught in English-speaking schools which were founded by Victorian colonialists, many Sikhs do not even possess the basic linguistic tools to recognize the subtleties of their sacred text. The verses of their Gurus may continually be seen, read and heard at all important occasions, during all rites of passage — without their import being really understood. I hope the present translations will open up their own literary tradition to them.

I also hope that these translations will be useful for those outside of the Sikh tradition. It will enable them to have an active dialogue with Sikhism. The Guru Granth provides an excellent example of going beyond particular affiliations and loyalties into the universal basis of religion. "There is One Being, Truth by Name" forms the fundamental principle of Sikh scripture. The Sikh vision of the Ultimate encompasses and transcends all space, time and gender, and cannot be imaged in any specific form. Such a perception shatters narrow and rigid barriers between peoples and makes possible an inclusive attitude towards followers from different religious and racial backgrounds. The thought that our multicultural and diverse world could benefit from Sikh views through these simple and accessible translations makes it a worthwhile venture.

On the other hand, the cultural differences make the job of translation a complex one. In spite of the Indo-European linguistic connections, there are some intrinsic differences between the East and the West. Translation of Sikh poetry into English meets with some basic problems. For example, in the Sikh worldview, emotions and thoughts are not bifurcated and we often hear the Sikh Gurus saying "we think with our hearts". Now how do we translate it without deviating from the original or sounding incomprehensible in English? Similarly in Sikh literature, "being the dust of feet" denotes being humble. To this day, Sikhs clean the dust off the shoes of other congregation members as a mark of humility and devotion. But a literal translation of "being the dust of feet" sounds strange in a culture which prides itself on individuality. In a society in which the norm is to shake hands and grandly introduce oneself, touching the feet of those whom we respect, or becoming the dust of their feet, sound rather eccentric. Another interesting phrase frequently found in the verse of the Sikh Gurus is var var, literally, going round and round sacrificing ourself to the cherished object. When we fall in love, we do go in circles! But instead of reckoning it a silly childish act, the Sikh Gurus hold it in very high esteem. The love for the Transcendent is idealized by them in the fullness of this very experience: ecstatic, we go beyond ourself; totally devoted to our Object, we go round and round. Indeed, the process of translation while showing us the universality also reveals the particularities of the human imagination.

To compound matters, the English language carries its own set of impositions. Many of its important terms are imbued with Jewish and Christian meaning. When such terms are used for rendering Sikh verse, how does the translator ensure that the readers stay clear of their Western connotations? Clearly, the role of the translator is not that of an interpreter, and, though there is the urge to explain, the translator has to keep to his or her own obligations, that is remain as close as possible to the text — no additions; no subtractions. For the most part the original verse lends itself to English quite well and it surprises me that translators in the past had to resort so excessively to words laden with Jewish and Christian connotations. I discovered that I could easily transit between Gurmukhi (the written script of Punjabi) and English without having to use terms like "God", "Lord" and "Soul" which were quite unnecessary and actually distorted the essential meaning. For example the term "soul" immediately brings to mind a bipartite framework, one in which the body is not only subordinated to the soul but also given a negative identity. Sikh literature straightforwardly establishes an identity between spiritual light and physical body: eka joti joti hai sarira[2] — "there is one light and the light is also the body". The self is the body; the self is the spirit, and a bodiless soul is certainly not demarcated as primary in this case. The important distinction in Sikhism however is that of the *self* cognizant of its essence versus the *self* ignorantly turned towards its ego rather than a distinction between two separate entities, body and soul. The cognizant self and the ignorant self are not separate entities, they are the self-same thing. To translate as "soul" would be highly misleading.

In the past translators used "God" for the various divine names, and "Lord" for sahib but there is no reason to follow

---

[2] Guru Granth p. 125.

their practice. "God" as explained by Mary Daly is a reified noun which takes away the dynamism of the verb Be-ing.[3] In the conception of God we see the omnipotent Reality standing up and above. In the Sikh conception, however, the supreme reality is utterly transcendent and intimately present "within each and every heart" (ghati, ghati) as the Sikh Gurus reiterate in their verse, so the usage of the term "God" is incongruous. Similarly, the use of the word "Lord" to translate sabib is inaccurate. The word "Lord" is masculine alone, an objection which does not apply to the inclusive term "Sovereign". Furthermore, a lord can be anything from the master of a tiny estate to the ruler of a country to the male God of Judaism and Christianity, whereas the term "Sovereign" emphasizes the supremacy of a completely independent ruler, male or female. By clinging to established translations we put words into a mould that destroys their vitality and we end up freezing our ideas and congealing our emotions.

The work of translation is made even more difficult in that the Sikh Gurus used Sanskrit and Arabic terms. Concepts like dharam which means "duty" in Sanskrit, or hukam, which means "will" in Arabic, are frequently used throughout the sacred text. Their usage signifies the liberal attitude of the Sikh Gurus who articulated their new message in terms that people in their day and age were familiar with. For the translator, however, their usage raises an important question: should the original terms be retained? In general I have chosen not to indicate any distinctions between words from Sanskrit or Arabic-Persian origin, and have translated them instead by their clearest English equivalent. This approach is closer to the spirit of the Gurus who wished to speak in a simple manner that would be readily

---

[3] Mary Daly, *Beyond God the Father : Toward a Philosophy of Women's Liberation.* Beacon Press, Boston, 1973.

accessible. They were using them not because of their Hindu or Islamic connotations but because they were concepts with which ordinary people were familiar. In fact, the meaning and significance of those concepts and terms in Sikh scripture varied considerably from their usage in Hindu and Islamic contexts. For example, the term Dharam retains its Sanskrit meaning ("what holds together") but its usage in Sikh scripture has a very different meaning from that of the Hindu ideal which regards the continuity of customary and conventional practices as dharma. The Sikh Gurus do not prescribe the customary fourfold caste division of Hindu society into priests, warrior-kings, traders and labourers, nor the four stages of life through chastity, family life, withdrawal and renunciation. In contrast, Sikh verse emphasizes equality in the practice of dharam; everyone is equally impelled to perform their ethical duty throughout their entire life.

A similar issue arises with divine Names. Although the Sikh Gurus abundantly use words such as Rama, Gobind, Hari, Narayan, Raghunath, these are not representative of Hindu avatars; they are poetic appellations for the Divine. In fact, Sikh texts categorically reject the doctrine of avtarvad. Guru Nanak says: "In comparison with the Fearless, Formless One, innumerable deities are as dust."[4] Or: "millions of Vishnus has It created, millions of universes has It spawned, millions of Shivas has It raised and assimilated."[5] The particularity and uniqueness of the Hindu gods, of any gods, is dismissed. Instead, the Sikh Gurus stressed the universal Reality. Adhering to Guru Nanak's vision, Guru Arjan declares that the essence is the same: "Some call it Rama, some call it Khuda; some worship it as

---

[4] Guru Granth, p. 464.
[5] Ibid., p. 1156.
[6] Ibid., p. 885.

Vishnu, some as Allah."[6] The Gurus' use of multiple names suggests that the Ultimate Reality is essentially unfathomable and cannot be adequately designated in any singular way, but is open to a variety of personal experiences. The various names show the Gurus' inclusive approach to the ineffable Reality. But I felt it would be misleading for me to use these particular names in my translation. A reader not familiar with Sikh thought might misinterpret these names and import erroneous connotations from their role in Indian mythology. It is therefore much more in keeping with the orientation of the Sikh Gurus to avoid these specific names in translation and adopt instead all-inclusive universal terms such as the One or the Divine. This is what I have done in my work except where a historical reference required the use of a specific name. Those names and Indian terms that do appear in the translation are explained in the glossary at the back of the book.

My greatest challenge by far has been to reveal fully the aesthetic dimension of Sikh literature. In the final verse of the Guru Granth (Mundavani), Guru Arjan underscores the artistic efficacy of the holy volume:

> In the platter three things lie:
> truth, contentment, contemplation.
> They contain the ambrosial Name,
> by which we are all sustained.
> They who eat, they who savour,
> they are liberated.[7]

The sacred scripture is therefore seen as a sumptuous platter (thal) full of delicacies, namely truth, contentment and contemplation, containing the ambrosial Name. According to

---

[7] *The Name of My Beloved*, p. 137.

Guru Arjan, then, the sacred verse offers the food which sustains us. It is the food of knowledge: the fundamental essence of the universe is perceived through it. It offers the food of contentment: the dissatisfied appetite, the hunger for more and more is fulfilled by it. It offers the food of contemplation: the flickering psyche, the ever-fluctuating thoughts are harmoniously anchored by hearing and reflecting upon its verses. But the "food" is not merely to be eaten; rather, as Guru Arjan says, it should also be savoured. Not through elaborate conceptualizing, but through a full and rich relishing of the sacred poetry, the individual obtains liberation from all finite confinements and from the ever-continuing cycle of birth and death. The poetry of love and devotion is to be approached with reverent wonder; it cannot be pried into with mere intellect. The verses of the Sikh Gurus come with their own speedy metre and cadence. As the Gurus said, they had no control over the flow of their utterances. From the very outset, they regarded their communication as divinely inspired. Full and sensuous, the words were further energized by the musical measures. The poetic dynamism of the Sikh sacred literature comes from the presence of alliteration, assonance, consonance, the constant repetition, symmetry and rhythm which creates a momentum so that the readers, hearers, singers go beyond themselves and are launched on a journey towards the Absolute One. In keeping with the message of the Sikh Gurus, their poetry has to be savoured. Taste is a difficult sense to transmit from one tongue to another. The fulfilment of such an obligation makes the task of translation exacting.

The Selections in this Book

Selections for translation have been chosen from both the Guru Granth and the Dasam Granth. They begin with the morning prayers from the Guru Granth, first and foremost the Jap (respectfully called Japji) by Guru Nanak which also begins the Guru Granth. Next, the Shabad Hazare which includes poetry by both Guru Nanak and Guru Arjan, the Fifth Guru. Although there is no rigid timing, these prayers, along with Jaap and Savayye from the Dasam Granth of Guru Gobind Singh, are traditionally said around sunrise.

After these come Rahiras and Kirtan Sohila which are recited in the evening. Rahiras combines poetry in the Guru Granth from four different Gurus as well as from the Dasam Granth of the Tenth Guru. Kirtan Sohila, said last thing before going to bed, is also a combination of different Gurus' verses from the Guru Granth.

VERSES OF THE SIKH GURUS

Portrait of Guru Nanak holding a book.
Faizabad or Lucknow, circa 1770. Kapany Collection.

Jap

JAP, respectfully known as Japji, was composed by Guru Nanak. It is the first prayer in the Guru Granth, and encapsulates the fundamental philosophical and ethical beliefs of the Sikhs. It is recited at the break of dawn when the mind is fresh and the atmosphere is serene. Described as the ambrosial hour in the Jap, dawn is considered most conducive to grasping the divine Word. Reading or reciting or hearing the Jap enables Sikhs to conceive the Formless Reality and instils in them an urge to unite with the Infinite One.

There is One Being
Truth by Name
Primal Creator
Without fear
Without enmity
Timeless in form
Unborn
Self-existent
The grace of the Guru.

MEDITATE
Truth before time
Truth throughout time
Truth here and now
Says Nanak, Truth is evermore.

1 Thought cannot think,
    nor can a million thoughts.
Silence cannot silence,
    nor can seamless contemplation.
Greed is not made greedless,
    not by the wealth of all the world.
Though a thousand mental feats become a million,
    not one can go with us.
How then to be true?
    How then to break the wall of lies?

51

By following the Will.
Says Nanak, this is written for us.

2   By the divine Will, all forms were created;
        what that Will is, no one can say.
    By that Will, all life is formed
        and, by that Will, all are exalted.
    The Will determines what is high and what is low;
        the Will grants all joy and suffering.
    Some are blessed by the Will,
        others migrate from birth to birth.
    All are within the Will, none stands apart.
    Says Nanak, by recognizing the Will,
        we silence our ego.

3   Filled with might, they sing praise of the Might,
    Seeing the signs, they sing praise of the Bounty,
    Perceiving the virtues, they sing praise of the Glory.
    Some sing praise through high philosophy,
    Some sing praise of the power that creates and destroys,
    Some sing in awe of the giving and taking of life.
    Some sing of the thereness, the utter transcendence,
    Some sing of the hereness, the close watch over all.
    Stories and stories add one to another,
    Preaching and preaching lead nowhere.
    The Giver gives, the receivers tire of receiving;
    Age upon age they eat and eat the gifts.
    All are directed by that Will;
    Says Nanak, the Carefree is ever in bliss.

4   The True Sovereign, Truth by Name,
        infinite love the language.
    Seekers forever seek gifts

and the Giver gives more and more.
What can we offer for a glimpse of the Court?
What can we say to win divine love?
In the ambrosial hour, exalt and reflect upon the True Name.
Through actions each is dressed in a body,
    but liberation comes only from the Gaze of grace.
Says Nanak, know the Absolute thus.

5   That One cannot be moulded or made,
Alone immaculate and self-existent.
Those who serve receive honours.
Nanak says, sing of the Treasure of virtues,
Sing, listen, and hold love in the heart
So sorrow is banished, joy ushered in.
Through the Guru comes the sacred Word,
    through the Guru comes the scripture,
    through the Guru, That One is experienced in all.
The Guru is Shiva, the Guru is Vishnu, the Guru is Brahma,
    the Guru is Parvati, Laxmi and Sarasvati.[1]
Were I to comprehend, I'd still fail to explain,
    for That One is beyond all telling.
Guru, let me grasp this one thing:
All creatures have one Provider,
    may I not forget this.

6   I would bathe at a pilgrimage site only to please That One;
    without approval what is the use?
I see the expanse of creation,
    how could it be without divine favour?

---

[1] The cycle of existence is represented through the Hindu trinity of the gods of creation, preservation and destruction and their respective consorts, the goddesses of knowledge, prosperity and energy. See Glossary.

Hearing a single teaching from the Guru,
  the mind shines with jewels, rubies and pearls.
Guru, let me grasp this one thing:
All creatures have one Provider,
  may I not forget this.

7 If we were to live four ages, or even ten times four,
  If we were known in the nine continents,
    and hailed as leader by all,
  If we were to win good name, glory and fame
    throughout the world,
  But were denied the loving Gaze, we would be cast out,
  Treated as the lowest of worms, accused as criminals.
  Says Nanak, the wicked are made virtuous,
    and the virtuous granted more virtue,
  But it is unthinkable that anyone could grant virtue to
    That One.

8 By hearing, we are graced like saints and gods,[2]
  By hearing, we fathom the earth, underworld and skies,
  By hearing, we know the nine continents,
    the many worlds and underworlds,
  By hearing, we are freed from the clutches of death.
  Says Nanak, the devout enjoy eternal bliss,
  Hearing banishes all suffering and sin.

9 By hearing, we become as Shiva, Brahma and Indra,
  By hearing, the corrupt open their mouths in praise,
  By hearing, ways of meditation and mysteries
    of the body are revealed,

---

[2] The original, translated here as "saints", lists siddhas, naths, pirs, a mixture of Hindu and Muslim spiritual achievers. See Glossary.

By hearing, treatises and scriptures are illumined.
Says Nanak, the devout enjoy eternal bliss,
Hearing banishes all suffering and sin.

10 Hearing leads to truth, contentment and knowledge,
Hearing bathes us in the sixty-eight sacred sites,
Hearing wins scholarly repute,
Hearing inspires peaceful contemplation.
Says Nanak, the devout enjoy eternal bliss,
Hearing banishes all suffering and sin.

11 Hearing the Word, we plumb the depths of virtue,
Hearing the Word, we rise to the status of sages and kings,
Hearing the Word, the path is lit for the blind,
Hearing the Word, the fathomless is fathomed.
Says Nanak, the devout enjoy eternal bliss,
Hearing the Word banishes all suffering and sin.

12 No words can speak of remembrance,
Attempts to explain are later regretted.
No paper, pen or scribe can describe,
Nor any philosophizing help to realize,
So wondrous is the immaculate Name,
It is known only by those who hold It in their mind.

13 Remembering, our mind and intellect awaken,
Remembering, we learn of all the worlds;
Remembering, we are safe from blows and pain;
Remembering, we part company with death.
So wondrous is the Immaculate Name,
It is known only by those who hold It in their mind.

14 Remembering, we walk on a clear path,

Remembering, we advance in honour and glory,
Remembering, we do not stray down lanes and byways,
Remembering, we keep to righteousness.
So wondrous is the Immaculate Name,
It is known only by those who hold It in their mind.

15 Remembering, we find the door to liberation,
Remembering, our family is liberated too,
Remembering, we swim and lead our companions
    to the shore,
Remembering, says Nanak, we need not beg
    in circles for freedom.
So wondrous is the Immaculate Name,
It is known only by those who hold It in their mind.

16 The chosen win approval, they are the chosen ones,
The chosen receive honours in the Court,
The chosen shine splendidly at the royal Gate,
The chosen meditate on the one and only Guru.
To speak or think of the Creator's deeds
Is beyond calculation.
The bull that bears the earth is righteousness,
    child of compassion,
Its rope is contentment, holding the earth in balance.
All who see, live the life of truth.
How heavy the weight borne by the bull,
For there is not one earth but many more above and beyond.
Who stands beneath supporting all?
This diversity of creatures, castes and colours
Has all been written in a single stroke of the Pen.
Who knows to write this infinite Writ?
What an infinite Writ to write.
What power and beauty of form.

How to estimate the gift,
This expanse from a single command,
Millions of rivers flowing forth at once.
How can I express the Primal Power?
I cannot offer myself to You even once,
Only that which pleases You is good.
You are for ever constant, Formless One.

17 Countless are the ways of meditation,
     and countless the avenues of love,
Countless the ways of worship,
     and countless the paths of austerity and sacrifice.
Countless the texts, and countless the Vedic reciters,
Countless the yogis turning away from the world,
Countless the devout reflecting on virtue and knowledge,
Countless the pious, and countless the patrons,
Countless the warriors, faces scarred by iron
Countless the sages sunk in silent trance.
How can I express the Primal Power?
I cannot offer myself to you even once.
Only that which pleases You is good.
You are for ever constant, Formless One.

18 Countless the fools lost in pitch dark,
Countless the thieves living off others,
Countless the tyrants bullying their way,
Countless the killers with blood on their hands,
Countless the sinners trailing misdeeds behind them,
Countless the liars spinning in lies,
Countless the perverts devouring filth,
Countless the slanderers bent by their burden.
After thought, lowly Nanak says this,
I cannot offer myself to you even once.

Only that which pleases You is good.
You are for ever constant, Formless One.

19 Countless are Your names and countless Your places,
Unreachable and unfathomable are Your countless spheres.
Declaring them "countless" we increase our burden.
Yet, by words we name, by words we acclaim,
By words we know and sing and praise,
By words we speak and by words we write,
By words we communicate and unite,
By words all our actions are written.
But who writes is above all writing.
As it is spoken, so are all allotted.
As expansive the creation, so too the Name,
There is no place without the Name.
How can I express the Primal Power?
I cannot offer myself to you even once.
Only that which pleases You is good.
You are for ever constant, Formless One.

20 Dirty hands, feet and body
Are washed clean with water.
Urine-stained clothes
Are washed with soap as well.
The mind polluted by evil
Is cleansed by the brilliance of the Name.
Good and evil are not mere words,
For our actions are written and go with us,
We reap only what we sow,
Nanak says, by the Will we come and go.

21 Any merit from pilgrimage, austerity, mercy and charity
Is barely worth a sesame seed.

Hearing, remembering and loving the Name
Immerses us in the sacred fount within.
Every virtue rests in You, I have none in me,
Without virtue, devotion is impossible.
Salutations! You are the world, the Word, the Creator,
You are Truth, You are Beauty, You are Joy Eternal.
What was the time, what was the hour,
What was the date, what was the day,
What was the season, what was the month,
When creation was born?
Had pundits the answer, it would be written
    in the Puranas,
Had qadis the answer, it would be written
    in the Qur'an,
No ascetic knows the date or day, no one knows
    the month or season.
The Creator who designed this creation alone knows.
How can I speak of You? How can I praise You?
    How can I describe You? How can I know You?
Nanak says, many speak of You, each outdoing the other.
Great is the Sovereign, great is Its Name, all that happens
    is Its doing,
Says Nanak, but those who claim credit stay unadorned
    in the hereafter.

22 Worlds below worlds, worlds above worlds,
    Tired of seeking their limits, the Vedas say one thing,
    Arabic scriptures speak of eighteen thousand worlds
        traced to one source.
    If It could be written, It would be written,
        but the writing passes.
    Nanak says, praise the Great who alone knows Itself.

23 Extollers extol but cannot fathom You,
   Like brooks and streams that flow to the ocean,
      nor knowing its expanse.
   Kings and sultans may rule kingdoms vast as oceans,
      possess wealth piled high as mountains,
   Yet none can match an ant who does not forget in her heart.[3]

24 Infinite is Your glory, and infinite the ways to sing
      Your praise,
   Infinite are the deeds, and infinite the gifts,
   Infinite is the seeing, and infinite the hearing,
   And infinite are the workings of That Mind.
   Infinite is the variety of forms,
   Infinite are the edges of the universe.
   And how many yearn to comprehend the limits?
   Even their end is not to be found.
   The end eludes all,
   The more it is expressed, the farther it extends.
   The Sovereign is great and high in station,
   Yet higher still is the Name.
   If we could ever reach that height,
   Then only would we know the Highest of the high.
   Expansive as It is, That One alone can know Itself.
   Nanak says, we are graced with the gift of the Gaze.

25 Grace abounds beyond all reckoning,
   Great is the Giver, with no trace of greed.
   How many great heroes beg from You
   And how many more, we cannot know.
   Many exhaust themselves in vicious deeds,

---

[3] The word here translated as "heart" is man, which signifies both thought (mind) and feeling (heart).

Many receive but deny their Giver,
Many fools eat and eat,
Many are devoured by pain and greed,
Yet these are borne as Your blessings, Giver.
Your Will frees us from bondage,
No one here can intercede,
The fool who dares speak
Alone knows the blows on his face.
That One alone knows, That One alone gives,
But few acknowledge this.
The person gifted to praise and adore,
Nanak says, is truly monarch of monarchs.

26 Priceless are the virtues, priceless their trade,
Priceless are the dealers, priceless the treasures in store,
Priceless are they who come for this trade,
    priceless what they take away,
Priceless is love, priceless those immersed in it,
Priceless is the law, and priceless the court,
Priceless are the scales, priceless the weights,
Priceless is the bounty, priceless the seal,
Priceless is the favour, priceless the command,
How priceless the Priceless One is, no one can say,
Those who try are lost in silence.
Vedas and Puranas have also sought to say,
Scholars say in their texts and discourses,
Brahmas say, Indras say,
Gopis and Krishnas say,
Shivas say, Siddhas say,
Innumerable Buddhas say,
The demons say, the gods say,
The virtuous, wise and devout say.
How many speak and begin to speak,

Many have spoken and gone,
And if their numbers were doubled again,
Still no one could say.
That One is as great as It chooses to be,
Nanak says, only the True One knows Itself.
That babbler who presumes to say
Is marked as the fool of fools.

27 What kind of a gate is it, what kind of a mansion
    where You sit and support all creation?
Countless are the instruments and melodies,
    countless the players singing Your praise,
Countless are the rags and their harmonies,
    countless the singers.
Wind, water and fire sing Your praise,
    at Your doorstep Dharmaraja sings Your praise,
His attendants, Chitra and Gupta, recording every deed
    while he checks their records, sing Your praise,
Shiva, Brahma and the Goddess, radiant with splendour
    bestowed by You, sing Your praise
Indra, seated upon his throne in a circle of gods,
    sings Your praise.
Siddhas in their meditation and sages in contemplation
    sing Your praise.
Celibates, saints and the serene sing Your praise,
    invincible heroes sing Your praise.
Scholars and great seers with their texts in every age
    sing Your praise.
Beautiful women, enchanting the mind in the celestial,
    terrestrial and nether worlds, sing Your praise.
Jewels that come from You, sites made sacred by You,
    sing Your praise.
Heroes and mighty warriors sing Your praise,

the four sources of life sing Your praise,
Continents, constellations, and universes upheld by You
sing Your praise.
Devotees who win Your affection, revelling in Your love,
sing Your praise.
How many other singers and players I cannot conceive.
Says Nanak, how then can I think of them?
That One, ever True Sovereign,
true is the praise of that True One.
That One is, ever will be,
and never will that Creator of the world not be.
Designer of this colourful diversity,
Creator of this variegated world,
You watch over and sustain Your creation,
all praise belongs to You.
Whatever You desire comes to pass,
none can challenge Your commands.
Nanak says, You are the Sovereign of sovereigns,
all abide by Your Will.

28 Wear contentment as your yogi earrings,
let honest actions be your pouch and begging bowl,
make inner contemplation your penitential ashes.
Death shall be the cloak you wear,
pure living your yogic discipline,
and faith the staff you lean upon.
Accept all humans as your equals,
and let them be your only sect.
Conquering ourselves, we conquer the world.
Salutations!
Salutations to That One who is primal, immaculate,
immortal, immutable, constant throughout the ages.

29 With knowledge as the banquet, compassion as the hostess,
  let the sacred music resonate in every heart.
The One is supreme, the whole cosmos under Its sway,
  why revere feats and miracles which lead you astray?
Meeting and parting are the rhythm of the universe,
  to all is given what is written.
Salutations!
Salutations to That One Who is primal, immaculate,
  immortal, immutable, constant throughout the ages.

30 Our mother, the visible world, gave birth alone to three sons.
The Creator, the Sustainer and one who holds the Court.
But everything goes as That One decrees,
  and all are under divine Command.
It watches over all, and, marvel of marvels,
  remains invisible to all.
Salutations!
Salutations to That One who is primal, immaculate,
  immortal, immutable, constant throughout the ages.

31 Its dwelling is in every realm. So too Its treasures.
Whatever is there was placed once and for all time.
After making, the Maker regards Its creation.
Nanak says, the works of the True One are for ever true.
Salutations!
Salutations to That One who is primal, immaculate,
  immortal, immutable, constant throughout the ages.

32 If one tongue became a hundred thousand tongues,
  and each of these became twenty times more,
And all recited it a hundred thousand times,
  the Owner of the world has but one Name.
The stairs to union are climbed without ego.

Hearing of those who reach these heights,
even the lowest are stirred to imitate.
Nanak says, the Gaze is received,
the boasting of the false is false.

33 It is not ours to speak or stay silent,
It is not ours to ask or give,
It is not ours to live or die,
It is not ours to gain riches that rattle the mind,
It is not ours to have consciousness,
knowledge and reflection,
It is not ours to be liberated from the cycle of life and death.
The One, whose power it is, regards Its doing.
Nanak says, no one is high or low.

34 Amid nights and seasons, dates and days,
Amid air, water, fire and netherworlds,
The earth is placed, the place for righteous action.
In it are colourful beings and lifestyles,
Infinite are their names and infinite their forms.
We are judged on every action performed;
The One is true, Its verdicts truly just.
Those who are accepted become radiant,
They glow with the mark of grace.
The raw and the ripened,[4]
Nanak says, reaching there, become known.

35 Such is the order of the Realm of Duty,
Now tell us about the Realm of Knowledge.
How many airs, waters and fires,
how many Krishnas and Shivas!

---

[4] A metaphor for the good and bad.

How many Brahmas, and in what variety of forms, colours
and guises they are created!
How many earths and mountains to live and act in,
how many saints, like Dhru, and their sermons!
How many Indras, moons and suns,
how many continents and universes!
How many ascetics, enlightened ones and yogic masters,
how many goddesses!
How many gods, demons and sages,
how many jewels and oceans!
How many species, how many languages
and how many rulers and kings!
How many revelations, how many devotees!
Says Nanak, there is no end to their end.

36 In the Realm of Knowledge, knowledge blazes forth,
Here reign mystic melodies and myriad sports and joys.
Now the Realm of Beauty is beauty itself,
Here the faculties are honed in unmatched splendour.
Words fail to describe,
They who try lament their lack.
Here consciousness, wisdom, mind and discernment
are honed,
Awareness sharpened like that of the gods and mystics.

37 The Realm of Grace is full of force,
Here is the One with no other.
Here heroes and mighty warriors dwell,
Inspired by Rama.
Here are Sita and women of her fame and virtue,
Their beauty beyond words.
They do not die, they are not beguiled,
For Rama is in their hearts.

Saints from many worlds live in this Realm of Grace.
They know bliss, for the True One
  is imprinted on their minds.
In the Realm of Truth, the Formless One is at home,
Gazing upon Its creation.
Here are continents, constellations, and universes
Whose limits cannot be told.
Here are creatures of various forms,
All acting according to the Will.
That One watches, rejoices
  and contemplates Its own creation.
Nanak says, to describe this is as hard as iron.

38 Let continence be your smithy, and patience your goldsmith.
Let wisdom be your anvil, and knowledge your hammer.
Let awe be the bellows, and inner control the blazing fire.
In the crucible of love, let the ambrosia flow,
In this true mint, forge the Word,
Such fulfilment comes to those blessed with the Gaze.
Says Nanak, happy are they who are gazed upon.

EPILOGUE
Air is our Guru, water our father,
  and the great earth our mother.
Day and night are the female and male nurses
  in whose laps the whole universe plays.
Good and bad deeds are all disclosed
  in the presence of Righteousness.
Our actions take us near or far.
Those who remember the Name earn true success.
Nanak says their faces shine,
  and they take many with them to liberation.

Shabad Hazare

SHABAD HAZARE, literally "Thousand Words", is recited in the morning, along with the Jap. It is a combination of poetic pieces from different Gurus in different rags or melodic frameworks, which are therefore found in different sections of the Guru Granth. The rag to which each piece is set and the Guru who composed it are indicated in its title (for further details of the organisation and reference system of the Guru Granth, see pp. 25-6).

Through feminine thoughts and feelings, the hymn expresses the yearning for the One, and tells us how to unite with That One. The male Gurus who composed these verses identify with the female and use her acts of dressing and putting on perfume for her lover to fully develop the nuance of intimacy and passion in the human relationship with the Divine.

Majh Mahalla 5

1   My mind pines for a vision of the Guru,
It wails like the chatrik bird.
My thirst is unquenched, and I find no peace
    without sight of the beloved saint.

May I offer myself again and again
    for a vision of the beloved and holy Guru.

2   Your face is beautiful, and the music of Your sweet
Word brings peace within.
It has been so long since I caught a glimpse of You,
    I yearn for You as a soaring bird for water.
Blessed is the land where You dwell,
    my good and beloved Friend.

May I offer myself again and again,
    my Guru, my good and beloved Friend.

3   A moment without sight of You passes painfully
    as a long dark age.
When shall I see you now, my blessed Beloved?
My nights are a torment, I cannot sleep a wink
    without a glimpse of the Court.

May I offer myself again and again

to the True One's Court.

4   By good fortune I have met the holy Guru,
And I have found the Immortal in my own house.
May I always serve You,
    never parting for a minute
    or moment, Nanak is Your humble slave.

May I offer myself again and again,
    Nanak is Your humble slave.

Dhanasri Mahalla 1

1   My heart trembles, whom shall I call?
I should devote myself to the Healer of suffering,
    the One who is ever and ever the Giver.

My Sovereign is always fresh,
    and ever and ever the Giver.

2   Night and day, we must serve the Sovereign,
    the One who will liberate us at last.
Hearing the Word, my sisters,
    we reach the other shore.

Compassionate One, by contemplating Your Name,
    we swim to the shore of liberation.
    I offer myself to You a hundred times.

3   The True One is everywhere,
    there is no other.
They serve, on whom the Gaze falls.

How can I live without You, my Beloved?

Grant me the honour of living in Your Name,
There is no other to whom I can turn, my Dearest.

4   Let me devote myself to You, my Sovereign,
        and look to no other.
    Nanak says, I am That One's slave,
        at every moment I offer myself, every bit of me.

To Your Name, my Sovereign,
    at every moment I offer myself, every bit of me.

Tilang Mahalla 1

1   This body of mine is steeped in illusion,
        the clothes I wear are dyed with greed.
    My Beloved does not like my dress,
        how then can this bride enter the nuptial bed?

I offer myself to You, Compassionate One,
    I offer myself to You.
I offer myself even to those who remember Your Name.
To those who remember Your Name,
    I offer myself a hundred times.

2   If my body were a vat, and the crimson of the Name
        were poured into it,
    And if the dyer were my Sovereign,
        such a brilliant colour would never have been seen.

3   Those who wear clothes so dyed,
        have the Beloved ever close to them.
    This is Nanak's plea,
        may I receive the dust of their feet.

4   That One creates, That One colours,
        That One bestows the loving Gaze.
    Nanak says, if a woman pleases the Husband
        then the Beloved makes love to her.

Tilang Mahalla 1

1   My naive one, why are you so vain?
    Why not celebrate the colours within your own house?
    The Bridegroom is very close to you,
        so, my silly girl, why search outside?
    If you paint your eyes with the eyeliners of fear,
        and adorn yourself with love,
    Then you will be the true bride
        with whom the Groom will stay in love.

2   Silly girl!
        What can she do if the Groom does not love her?
    She may despair and lament in many ways
        but she will not be admitted to the Mansion.
    Without good deeds we gain nothing
        however hard we run.
    Drunk with avarice, greed and arrogance,
        and drowned in illusion,
    You will never reach the Bridegroom so, my naive woman.

3   Go now to the true brides,
        ask them the way to reach the Bridegroom.
    "Whatever the One does, accept as good,
        and cast aside all other attitudes and loyalties.
    Whichever love brings us to the Object,
        to that we cling.

Do whatever the Groom asks of you,
>   wear the fragrance of devotion in body and spirit."
The true brides say,
>   "This is the way, sister, to reach the Bridegroom."

4   If you lose your ego, then you gain the Groom,
>   no other cleverness will do.
When the Bridegroom casts the loving Gaze, that day is
>   recorded, and the woman wins the nine treasures.
Loved by her Bridegroom, she is the true bride,
>   and she is the true sister of her brothers.
She is coloured by her Beloved,
>   immersed in tranquillity,
>   saturated with love day and night,
She is beautiful, she is radiant, she is brilliant,
>   and she is called wise.

Suhi Mahalla 1

1   Which scales, which weights,
>   which goldsmith should I call to assay You?
Which Guru should instruct me?
>   Whom should I approach to assess You?

My Beloved, I do not know your limits,
You pervade the earth, waters and the air above,
>   *You are ever present in all.*

2   If I were to use the scales of my mind,
>   the weights of my consciousness,
>   and the goldsmith of my service,
If I were to weigh You within myself,
>   then could I hold my consciousness in balance.

3   You are the indicator, You are the weight,
        You are the scales, and You are the assessor.
    You observe, You recognize,
        and You are the dealer.

4   The mind is ignorant, base and alienated,
        it flits from here to there.
    Nanak lives in such company,
        how can this fool ever find You?

Rag Bilaval Mahalla 1

1   It is no compliment if I call You a chief
        when You are our Sultan.
    I address You just as You direct me, my Guide,
        I am ignorant and do not know what to say.

    *Grant me the wisdom to sing Your glory
        and to abide in Truth, as is Your Will.*

2   Whatever happens is of Your doing,
        and all is known to You.
    I do not know Your limits, my Sovereign,
        I am ignorant, what cleverness have I?

3   What can I say?
        Whenever I try, I fail to express the Inexpressible.
    I can only say what pleases You,
        a sesame seed before Your greatness.

4   There are so many dogs and I am a stray one,
        I bark to appease the hunger of this body.

Nanak may lack devotion,
    but this cannot diminish the Husband's Name.

Bilaval Mahalla 1

1   If I make of my mind a temple,
       and of my body a hermit's robe,
       if I bathe in the fount of myself,
    If the One Word dwells in my breath,
       I will not return to the circle of life.

Mother, my mind is pierced
    with love for the Compassionate One.
But who can know another's pain?
The Divine is my only concern.

2   You who are unfathomable, unknowable,
       ineffable, infinite, do watch over us.
    You pervade the waters and the lands and the air above,
       Your Light shines in each and every heart.

3   All teaching, all wisdom, all enlightenment is Yours,
       all temples and shelters are Yours.
    My Sovereign, I know no one else but You,
       and I sing your glory forever.

4   All creatures seek refuge in Your lap,
       responsibility for all rests with You.
    Whatever pleases You is good,
       This is all Nanak has to say.

MORNING

Jaap

JAAP (with a long a) is a poetic offering to the Ultimate Reality. It is the obeisance to the Transcendent One by the Tenth Sikh Guru, Guru Gobind Singh, and is from the Dasam Granth (Book of the Tenth Guru). In 199 verses, it is a marvellous profusion of divine attributes that flashed on the Guru's artistic consciousness. He ends at verse 199 rather than at a round figure to signify that there is no culminating point. The outpouring of words saluting the Infinite Reality is dynamic, the rhythm most speedy, and so this morning prayer of the Sikhs becomes an important aesthetic medium for contemplating the Ultimate Reality.

1   You have no trait, no trace whatsoever,
       no colour, caste or family.
    How to describe Your features or complexion,
       the lines on Your palms or Your garb?
    You are called eternal, self-illumined, of infinite power,
    Supreme among countless deities, Ruler among rulers,
    Guardian of the three worlds—gods, humans and
       demons, tiny blades of grass and towering forests
       all proclaim Your infinity.
    Who can recount all Your names?
    The wise name You from Your actions.

2   Salutations to You, the Timeless
    Salutations to You, the Merciful
    Salutations to You, the Formless
    Salutations to You, the Incomparable

3   Salutations to You, the Unattired
    Salutations to You, the Inexpressible
    Salutations to You, the Bodiless
    Salutations to You, the Unborn

4   Salutations to You, the Invincible
    Salutations to You, the Indestructible
    Salutations to You, the Nameless
    Salutations to You, the Placeless

5 Salutations to You who are beyond all deeds
Salutations to You who are beyond all duties
Salutations to You who are beyond all names
Salutations to You who are beyond all places

6 Salutations to You, the Unbeatable
Salutations to You, the Fearless
Salutations to You, the Unyielding
Salutations to You, the Indomitable

7 Salutations to You, the Formless
Salutations to You, the Timeless
Salutations to You, the Impenetrable
Salutations to You, the Unfathomable

8 Salutations to You, the Invincible
Salutations to You, the Invulnerable
Salutations to You, the Generous
Salutations to You, the Boundless

9 Salutations to You, the Absolutely Single
Salutations to You, the Infinitely Countless
Salutations to You who are beyond the five elements
Salutations to You who are free of all entanglements

10 Salutations to You who are free of action
Salutations to You who are free of delusion
Salutations to You who are free of place
Salutations to You who are free of garb

11 Salutations to You, the Nameless
Salutations to You, the Desireless
Salutations to You, the Immaterial

Salutations to You, the Inviolable

12 Salutations to You, the Immovable
Salutations to You, the Insubstantial
Salutations to You, the Invisible
Salutations to You, the Unworried

13 Salutations to You who are beyond all suffering
Salutations to You who are beyond all depiction
Salutations to You who are honoured in the three worlds
Salutations to You who are our true Treasure

14 Salutations to You, the Unfathomable
Salutations to You, the Unshakable
Salutations to You, the All-encompassing
Salutations to You, the Unborn

15 Salutations to You, the Enjoyer of everything
Salutations to You, the Pervader of everyone
Salutations to You, the Colourless
Salutations to You, the Absolute

16 Salutations to You, the Incomprehensible
Salutations to You, the Beautiful
Salutations to You, the Supporter of oceans
Salutations to You, the Unsupported

17 Salutations to You, the Casteless
Salutations to You, the Kinless
Salutations to You, the Sectless
Salutations to You, the Wonderful

18 Homage to You who have no country

Salutations to You who have no vesture
Salutations to You who have no dwelling
Salutations to You, the Unborn

19 Salutations to You who bring death to all
Salutations to You who grant mercy to all
Salutations to You who permeate all
Salutations to You who rule us all

20 Salutations to You, our Annihilator
Salutations to You, our Creator
Salutations to You, our Destroyer
Salutations to You, our Sustainer

21 Salutations to You, the Luminous
Salutations to You, the Mysterious
Salutations to You, the Eternal
Salutations to You, the Most Beautiful

22 Salutations to You who have access to all
Salutations to You who exist everywhere
Salutations to You who contain all colours
Salutations to You who shatter all forms

23 Salutations to You, the Death of death
Salutations to You, the Compassionate
Salutations to You, the Colourless
Salutations to You, the Immortal

24 Salutations to You, the Ageless
Salutations to You, the Maker of all
Salutations to You, the Activator
Salutations to You, the Free

25   Salutations to You who have no kin
Salutations to You who fear no one
Salutations to You, the Merciful
Salutations to You, the Compassionate

26   Salutations to You, the Infinite
Salutations to You, the Greatest of all
Salutations to You, the Embodiment of Love
Salutations to You, the Most Fortunate

27   Salutations to the Annihilator
Salutations to the Nurturer
Salutations to the Creator
Salutations to the Destroyer

28   Salutations to the supreme Ascetic
Salutations to the supreme Reveller
Salutations to the Benevolent
Salutations to the Sustainer of all

29   Formless
Incomparable
Immovable
Transcendent

30   Without description
Without attire
Without name
Without desire

31   Inconceivable
Mysterious
Unassailable

Fearless

32   You are exalted in all three worlds
You are the precious Treasure
You encompass all three goals of life
You were never born

33   Infinite
No beginning
Invincible
No origin

34   Beyond birth
Beyond caste
Beyond matter
Beyond fetters

35   Unconquered
Unbreakable
Unchallenged
Unshakeable

36   Deep You are
Friend You are
Unencumbered
Utterly free

37   Enigmatic
Unknowable
Immortal
Unbound

38   Traceless

Placeless
Infinite
The Greatest

39   Without limits
Without kin
Totally independent
Utterly unknowable

40   Unreachable
Unborn
Insubstantial
Intangible

41   Beyond our vision
Above all worries
Beyond all actions
Above all superstitions

42   Unconquerable
Fearless
Firm as the mountains
Deep as the ocean

43   Immeasurable
Supreme Treasure
Of countless forms
Yet One

44   Salutations to the One revered by all
Salutations to the Treasure of all
Salutations to the God of gods
Salutations to the formless Mystery

45 Salutations to the Destroyer of death
   Salutations to the Preserver of all life
   Salutations to the One with access to all
   Salutations to the One present everywhere

46 Sovereign, You have no body
   Vanquisher, You need no ally
   Salutations to the Sun of suns
   Salutations to the Glory of glories

47 Salutations to the Moon of moons
   Salutations to the Sun of suns
   Salutations to the Song of songs
   Salutations to the Tune of tunes

48 Salutations to the Dance of dances
   Salutations to the Sound of sounds
   Salutations to the Hand of hands
   Salutations to the Reason of reason

49 Formless, nameless
   The beautiful universal Form
   Destroyer of all tyrants
   Bestower of all wealth and joy

50 Stainless
   Immaculate
   Salutations to the Ruler of rulers
   To the supreme Form

51 Salutations to the Yogi of yogis
   To the greatest Siddha
   Salutations to the King of kings

To the Greatest of the great

52   Salutations to the Wielder of weapons
     Salutations to the Hurler of missiles
     Salutations to the Knower of all
     Salutations to the Mother of the cosmos

53   Without form, without doubts
     Not seduced by senses, not weakened by temptation
     Salutations to You, the Yogi of yogis
     Salutations to the highest Way

54   Salutations to You, our constant Protector
     To the undaunted Vanquisher of evildoers
     Salutations to You, the Sustainer of gods and demons
     To the most Righteous

55   Salutations to the Dispeller of disease
     Salutations to the Incarnation of love
     Salutations to the Merchant of merchants
     Salutations to the Emperor of emperors

56   Salutations to the most Beneficent
     Salutations to the most Revered
     Salutations to the Dispeller of disease
     Salutations to You, the Bestower of purity

57   Salutations to You, the Sound of sounds
     Salutations to You, the Image of images
     Salutations to You, the Ground of our faith
     Salutations to You, the System of systems

58   Ultimate Truth, Consciousness and Bliss

Extinguisher of all
Incomparable, formless
Immanent in all

59　Giver of spiritual energy, Giver of mental power
Cause of all success
Pervader of the underworld, the earth and skies above
Destroyer of hosts of sins

60　Highest of the high
Unseen Giver of all we own
Power behind us all
Compassionate Giver

61　Impervious, impenetrable
Nameless, desireless
Conquerer of all
Present everywhere

62　In water
On land
Fearless
So mysterious

63　Almighty
Immutable
Without country
Without garb

64　Unfathomable, unboundable
Embodiment of bliss
Salutations to You who are honoured by all
Salutations to You who are the treasure of all

65   Salutations to You, the absolute Commander
     Salutations to You, the supreme Conqueror
     Salutations to You, the Invincible
     Salutations to You, the Indestructible

66   Salutations to You, the Timeless
     Salutations to You, the Autonomous
     Salutations to the One present in every land
     Salutations to the One present in every garb

67   Salutations to the King of kings
     Salutations to the Designer of designers
     Salutations to the Ruler of rulers
     Salutations to the Moon of moons

68   Salutations to the Song of songs
     Salutations to the Love of love
     Salutations to the Fury of furies
     Salutations to the Fire of fires

69   Salutations to the Inflicter of disease
     Salutations to the Enjoyer of everything
     Salutations to the Conqueror of all
     Salutations to the Terrifier of all

70   Salutations to the Omniscient
     Salutations to the Omnipotent
     Salutations to the supreme Sound
     Salutations to the supreme Image

71   Salutations to the One who watches us all
     Salutations to the One who attracts us all
     Salutations to the One who contains all colours

Formless, Annihilator of the three worlds

72 Salutations to the Life of all lives
Salutations to the Primal Seed
Serene and undaunting
Showering us all with gifts

73 Embodiment of compassion
Annuller of vice
Always and ever You remain
The source of spiritual energy

74 Whose work is immortal
Whose laws are immutable
The whole cosmos is yoked to You
Our eternal bliss

75 Whose rule is timeless
Whose creation is eternal
Whose laws are perfect
Whose deeds are unknown

76 Gracious Giver
Intimate Knower
Universal Enlightener
Revered by all

77 Life of all
Shelter to all
Relisher of all
Yoked with all

78 Deity of all

Knower of all
Death of all
Nurturer of all

79   Primal Form, timeless Profile, unborn, infinite Being,
      Divinity of the three worlds, extolled by all,
            unknown, primal, bountiful,
      Nourisher of all, Vanquisher of all, Destroyer of all,
      Omnipresent, most fervent Ascetic, most ardent Reveller.

80   Nameless, placeless, casteless,
            without form, colour or contour,
      Expansive timeless Being,
            unborn, primal, and absolute,
      Confined to no country or garb,
            to no form, shape or attachment,
      The Embodiment of Love
            extends to all lands, to every nook and cranny.

81   Nameless, desireless, our One alone has no place,
      Everyone, everywhere exalts You always,
      Your single form is seen in countless ways,
      Having played the sports of creation,
            You are for ever the One.

82   Gods cannot know You,
            nor scriptures of East or West,
      Your form, colour, caste are unknown,
            Your splendour for ever shines
      No father, no mother, no birth, no death,
      Your weapon whirls in all four directions,
            You are worshipped by all creatures.

83   In every layer of the world,
      all creatures contemplate the Name,
   Primal Being, timeless form,
      Foundation of this whole creation,
   Highest One, Immaculate One, absolute and infinite Being,
   Creator of the universe, self-existent, Sculptor and Shatterer.

84   Deathless and almighty, timeless and placeless,
   Full of virtue, devoid of doubt,
      insubstantial, invisible, formless,
   No body, attachment, or colour,
      no caste, lineage, or name,
   Vanquisher of pride and vice,
      Granter of freedom and Fulfiller of desires.

85   Self-manifesting, profound, beyond praise,
      Absolute Reality, utterly free,
   Dispeller of pride and evil, primal, unborn,
   Bodiless, eternal, not two, One, infinite,
   Omnipotent, Destroyer and Sustainer of us all.

86   Reaching and ending all, yet apart from each and all,
   No scripture knows Your form, colour or contour.
   The Vedas and Puranas all declare,
      You are the highest, You are unique,
   Yet countless scriptures fail to grasp You.

87   Mine of virtues, unending munificence
   Praise infinite
   Throne eternal
   Glory unequalled

88   Self-enlightened

Ever present
Long-reaching
Emperor of emperors

89   Ruler of rulers
Sun of suns
God of gods
Your glory is the greatest

90   Indra of Indras
Highest of the high
Poorest of the poor
Death of death

91   Immaterial Form
Immortal Light
Immeasurable, infinite
Mine of virtues and munificence

92   Hosts of ascetics worship You
Fearless and desireless One
Your brilliance is overpowering
Your glory unceasing

93   Your works are effortless
Your laws paradigmatic
You are our sole Sustainer
Who could reprimand You?

94   Protector
Saviour
Liberator
Infinite

95 Destroyer
    Creator
    Nameless
    Desireless

96 In all four directions, the Creator
    In all four directions, the Destroyer
    In all four directions, the Giver
    In all four directions, the Knower

97 Pervading in all four directions
    Supplying in all four directions
    Nurturing in all four directions
    Destroying in all four directions

98 In all four directions You are near
    In all four directions You abide
    In all four directions You are exalted
    In all four directions You shower gifts

99 With no enemy
    With no friend
    With no doubt
    With no fear

100 Free of action
    Free of body
    Free of birth
    Free of place

101 Without profile
    Without friend
    Distant from all

Purest of all

102 Sovereign of the earth
Its timeless Ruler
Invisible
Invincible

103 With place impenetrable
With garb impermeable
Nor won by rituals
Not moved by illusions

104 Of realm impermeable
Scorcher of the sun
Of colour immaculate
Deliverer of wealth and joy

105 Glory of kings
Flag of righteousness
Free from anxiety
Ornament most prized

106 Creator of the cosmos
Mightiest of the mighty
Supreme Being
Awareness most unique

107 Primal One, supreme Divinity
Unknown to all
Formless
Utterly autonomous

108 Universal Provider

Compassionate Liberator
Pure and immaculate
Totally unknowable

109 Forgiver of sins
Ruler of rulers
Cause of actions
Provider of food

110 Kind Provider
Gracious Giver
Full of power
Destroyer of all

111 Venerated everywhere
Showering gifts everywhere
Extending everywhere
Present everywhere

112 Dwelling in every country
Manifest in every form
Ruling every place
Creating all

113 Giving to everyone
Taking from everyone
Glory extending everywhere
Light illumining everything

114 Dwelling in every land
Manifest in every form
Destroying all
Nurturing all

115 Extinguishing all
Extending to all
Manifesting in all
Watching us all

116 All works
All majesty
All undoing
All protecting

117 Ever the power
Ever the breath
Dwelling in every country
Permeating every form

118 Exalted throughout
Supreme throughout
Contemplated throughout
Established throughout

119 Ever the sun
Ever exalted
Ever supreme
Ever the moon

120 Melodious speech
Highest understanding
Spiritual wisdom
Source of language

121 Acme of beauty
Attentive to all
Ever existing

Eternal Your creation

122 Destroyer of the enemy
Protector of the poor
Mansion on high
Ever present on earth

123 Totally aware
Richest Resource
Greatest Friend
Assured Provider

124 Infinite as the waves
Unknown, eternal
Cherisher of the devout
Chastiser of foes

125 Form ineffable
Free from elements
Brightest Radiance
Choicest Elixir

126 Immutable form
Inscrutable, incomparable
Ever victorious
Creator eternal

127 Ever perfect
Ever desireless
Insurmountable
Unfathomable, incomparable

128 Our Primal Being

Timeless Reality
Without body, without name
Sought by all three worlds

129 All-encompassing, all-controlling
Invincible, unfathomable
All Your forms are beautiful
All of us are loved by You

130 Rapture of the three worlds
Imperishable, intangible
Annuller of hell
Present everywhere

131 Of glory ineffable
Everlasting, eternal
Of varied forms
Yet incomparably One

132 Forever ineffable
Light in each and all
Of inexpressible Form
Yet incomparably One

133 Indestructible One
Without body
Without attire
Utterly inexpressible

134 Beyond doubts
Beyond deeds
Without beginning
Ever existing

135 Invincible
    Indestructible
    Insubstantial
    Unflinching

136 Free of destruction
    Free of attachment
    Free of conflict
    Free of all bonds

137 Absolute One
    Untrammelled
    Eternal
    Light

138 Carefree
    Eternal
    Ineffable
    Invisible

139 Indescribable
    Immaterial
    Immovable
    Immeasurable

140 Birthless
    Boundless
    Colourless
    Timeless

141 Unique
    Eternal
    Birthless

Primal

142 Killing all
Reaching all
Known to all
Knowing all .

143 Destroying all
Creating all
The breath of all
The power of all

144 All action
All virtue
Yoked to all
Free from all

145 Exalt the Annuller of hell
Exalt the perennial Light
Exalt the formless Form
Exalt Joy eternal

146 Vanquisher of villains
Our constant companion
Incomprehensible Form
Your joy can never be disrupted

147 Formless, nameless
Destroyer and Beloved of the three worlds
Eternal Form
Absolute, incomparable

148 Without children or grandchildren

Without friend or enemy
Without father or mother
Without caste or lineage

149 Without kin and competitors
With depth immeasurable
Of light eternal
Invincible, birthless

150 Ever visible Brilliance
Ever present
Ever preserved
Spoken of by all

151 Sovereign intellect
Lamp of beauty
Most compassionate
Merciful Nurturer of all

152 Giver of food
Deliverer of freedom
Most compassionate
Most beautiful

153 Crusher of the enemy
Supporter of the poor
Destroyer of foes
Dispeller of fears

154 Washing away our stains
Present in all
Unvanquished by enemies
Merciful nurturer of all

155 The speech of all
   The Sovereign of all
   Destroying all hells
   Dwelling in paradise

156 Reaching us all
   Always in bliss
   Recognizing us all
   Loved by all

157 Supreme Ruler
   Never visible
   Without country, without description
   Ever without form

158 On earth and in the skies
   Faith profound
   Beauty magnificent
   Power tremendous

159 Radiance eternal
   Fragrance inexhaustible
   Mystery magnificent
   Wealth uncountable

160 Endless Expanse
   Spiritual Light
   Immutable, immaterial
   Immeasurable, imperishable

161 Sages bow in their minds
   To the eternal Treasury of virtue
   Enemies cannot defeat

The Ruler and Destroyer of all

162 Millions pay homage
Sages bow their minds
Absolute Ruler
Glory supreme

163 Self-illumined, immortal
Enlightenment of the sages
Exalt the Treasury of virtues
Exalt the One ever present in water and on land

164 Eternal Form
Immutable Throne
Matchless Beauty
Endless Expanse

165 Glorious in water and on land
Unimpeachable anywhere
Greatest in water and on land
Infinite everywhere

166 Self-illumined, immortal
Your throne is the highest
Mighty One with outstretched arms
That One alone for ever

167 Primal Being
Whose origin cannot be told
You shatter evil in an instant
Mighty and timeless are You

168 Your glory resounds in every home

Your Name beats in every heart
Ageless Body
You are utterly independent

169 Ever stable
Never angry
Of endless bounty
Self-created, infinite

170 Invisible Your laws
Fearless Your works
Infinite, invulnerable
Greatest Giver

171 Abode of mercy
Conquerer of the enemy
Destroyer of evil
Designer of the earth

172 Sovereign of the world
Supreme Ruler
Shatterer of the evil
Protector of all

173 Sustainer of the earth
Creator of the world
Our hearts worship You
The world wishes to know You

174 You are our Preserver
You are our Creator
You are with us all
You are our Destroyer

175 Abode of compassion
    Nurse of the world
    Ruler of all
    Sovereign supreme

176 Life of the universe
    Destroyer of enemies
    Farther than the farthest
    Abode of mercy

177 Cannot be contained in a chant
    Cannot be reduced to an idol
    Cannot be captured in an image
    Immortal, the Elixir of elixirs

178 Elixir of elixirs
    Embodiment of mercy
    Unforgeable Form
    Supporter of the earth

179 Our supreme Elixir
    Our supreme Ruler
    Unforgeable Form
    Elixir of elixirs

180 Wonderful One
    Elixir of elixirs
    Sovereign of humanity
    Annuller of enemies

181 Preserver of the world
    Abode of mercy
    Ruler of rulers

Sustainer of all

182 You sunder the cycle of life and death
Conquerer of foes
Chastiser of enemies
Reminding us of Your Name

183 Immaculate One
Absolute One
Creator of the creator
Destroyer of the destroyer

184 The Transcendent Self
The Self within us all
Governing Your own Self
The Glory of glories

185 Salutations to the Sun of suns,
salutations to the Moon of moons,
Salutations to the Ruler of rulers,
salutations to the Deity of deities,
Salutations to the deep Darkness,
salutations to the brilliant Light,
Salutations to the largest Multitude,
salutations to the tiniest Seed.

186 Salutations to the Maker of passion,
inertia and truth,
Salutations to the subtlest Essence,
beyond the five elements,
Salutations to the Ascetic of ascetics,
Knowledge most excellent,
Salutations to the Word of words,

Contemplation most excellent.

187 Salutations to the Warrior of warriors,
   Knowledge most excellent,
Salutations to the Food of foods,
   the Drink of drinks,
Salutations to the Initiator of conflict,
   the Harbinger of peace,
Salutations to the Deity of deities,
   salutations to the timeless Treasure.

188 Immaculate One, Jewel amongst jewels,
Salutations to the Hope of hopes,
   salutations to the Beauty of beauties.
Indestructible, formless, nameless,
   Destroyer of the three worlds,
Existing in time past, present and future,
   without form, without desire.

189 Invincible
   Indomitable
   Fearless
   Immutable

190 Birthless
   Eternal
   Indestructible
   All-pervasive

191 Invincible
   Unyielding
   Invisible
   Unconsumed

192 Timeless
  Compassionate
  Ineffable
  Formless

193 Nameless
  Desireless
  Unattainable
  Ineradicable

194 Autonomous
  Destroyer
  Birthless
  Not silent

195 Without attachment
  Without colour
  Without form
  Without features

196 Beyond action
  Beyond doubt
  Beyond conquest
  Beyond depiction

197 Salutations to the Revered One
    who destroys us all,
  Salutations to the invincible Nameless One
    who exists everywhere,
  Salutations to the desireless Treasure
    who is manifest everywhere,
  Salutations to the Destroyer of evil
    who fosters goodness.

198 Forever truth, consciousness and bliss,
    vanquishing enemies,
Abounding in gifts, You create us all,
    You dwell in us all,
Of wondrous glory, furious against tyrants,
Our Destroyer, our Creator, full of benevolence,
    full of compassion.

199 Present in all four directions,
    rejoicing in all four directions,
Self-illumined, most beautiful, forever tied to each of us,
Freeing us from the pain of birth and death,
    Compassion itself,
For ever by our side, Radiance eternal.

Savayye

SAVAYYE means quatrains. The ten Savayye that have been included in the Sikhs' morning prayers are from Guru Gohind Singh's Dasam Granth (see p. 1). They underscore devotion as the essence of religion. They reject all forms of external worship and cast Guru Nanak's message of internal love in beautiful undulating rhythm. These Savayye are also recited during the administration of amrita, the initiation ceremony of the Khalsa (the Sikh order).

There is One Being. Victory to the wonderful Guru.
The composition of the Tenth Guru.
My wonderful Guru, I recite the Savayye by Your grace.

1   I have seen hosts of purists and ascetics,
        I have visited the homes of yogis and celibates.
    Heroes and demons, practitioners of purity
        and drinkers of ambrosia, hosts of saints
        from countless religions, I have seen them all.
    I have seen religions from all countries,
        but I have yet to see followers of the Creator.
    Without love for the Almighty,
        without grace from the Almighty,
        all practices are without a grain of worth.

2   Drunken elephants draped in gold,
        first among giants in blazing colours,
    Herds of horses, sprinting like gazelles,
        swifter than the wind,
    The people bow their heads to strong-armed rulers,
    But what if they be such mighty owners;
        at the last, they depart barefoot from the world.

3   Conquerors of the world march triumphant
        to the beat of kettle-drums.
    Their herds of handsome elephants trumpet,
        their royal steeds lustily neigh.

These rulers of past, future and present
    can never be counted.
Without worshipping the supreme Sovereign,
    all end in the house of death.

4   Pilgrimage, ablutions and charities, self-restraint
        and countless rituals,
    Study of Vedas, Puranas, Kateb and Qur'an,
        of all scriptures from all times and places,
    Ascetics subsisting on air, practising celibacy;
        countless such have I seen and considered.
    Without remembering the One, without love for the One,
        all rulers and actions go to naught.

5   Inured and invincible warriors in shining armour,
        determined to crush the enemy,
    Proudly think, mountains may grow wings and fly away,
        but never us.
    They can shatter their enemy, they can wring their foe,
        they can crush legions of drunken elephants,
    But without the grace of the One,
        they too must depart this world.

6   Countless heroes and doughty warriors
        who stand fast against the blows of iron,
    Who conquer lands and enemies,
        who crush the pride of drunken elephants,
    Who raze sturdy castles, who gain the world by words,
    They are all beggars at the divine Portal,
        the almighty Ruler is the only Giver.

7   Gods, demons, serpents, and ghosts contemplate
        Your Name in all time—past, present, and future.

All creatures of land and sea,
    You instantly create and destroy.
Their virtuous deeds are heartily celebrated,
    their piles of misdeeds utterly eradicated.
The devout go happily in this world,
    their enemies sink in shame.

8   Rulers of mortals and mighty elephants,
    leaders of the three worlds,
Performers of endless rituals and charities,
    winners of brides in countless swayamvara rites,
Like Brahma, Shiva, Vishnu and Sachi's husband,
    they all end at last in death.
They who touch the feet of the Transcendent One,
    they alone are freed from the cycle of birth and death.

9   How futile to sit in contemplation,
    like a stork with both eyes closed.
While trying to bathe in the seven seas,
    we lose this world and the next.
How futile to sink in misdeeds,
    we only waste away our life.
I tell the truth, do listen to me,
    they alone who love, find the Beloved.

10   Some worship stones, some bear them on their heads;
    some wear phalluses around their necks.
Some claim to see the One in the south;
    some bow their heads to the west.
Some worship idols, some images of animals;
    some run to worship the dead and their graves.
The entire world is lost in false ritual;
    none knows the mystery of the Almighty One.

Rahiras

RAHIRAS is part of the evening service. It consists of hymns by Guru Nanak (including, with a slight variation, stanza 27, Sodar, from the Jap), Guru Ram Das and Guru Arjan. Guru Gobind Singh's Chaupai Benati from the Dasam Granth also forms a part of this prayer. It concludes with pieces by Guru Amar Das including the first five stanzas and last stanza of his forty-stanza Anand ("Bliss"), a rapturous hymn focussing on the bliss that results from the individual's union with the Ultimate. In this abbreviated form, Anand is very popular. It is liturgically recited at the conclusion of all congregational services and joyful ceremonies such as weddings and name-giving. In Rahiras, the six stanzas of Anand are followed by Guru Arjan's Mundavani ("Seal") which concludes the entire Guru Granth. This evening prayer ends with Shalok ("Couplet"), also by Guru Arjan. A number of the hymns have a chorus which is placed after the first stanza in italics.

Year round, the Sikhs recite Rahiras just as day and night come together during the reflective period of dusk. Through the

Rahiras, the Sikhs pay homage to the Transcendent Reality, they sing praise of the divine Magnificence, they seek the protection and succour of the omnipotent Creator, and they express their joy upon hearing the melodious Word within their inner self. (Begins on p. 8 in Guru Granth.)

Sodar Rag Asa Mahalla 1

What kind of gate leads to You? What kind of mansion
    have You, where You sit and support all creation?
Countless are the instruments and melodies,
    countless the players singing Your praise,
Countless are the rags and their harmonies,
    countless the singers.
Wind, water and fire sing Your praise,
    at Your doorstep Dharmaraja sings Your praise,
His attendants, Chitra and Gupta, recording every deed
    while he checks their records, sing Your praise,
Shiva, Brahma and the Goddess, radiant with splendour
    bestowed by You, sing Your praise
Indra, seated upon his throne in a circle of gods,
    sings Your praise.
Siddhas in their meditation and sages in contemplation
    sing Your praise.
Celibates, saints and the serene sing Your praise,
    invincible heroes sing Your praise.
Scholars and great seers with their texts in every age
    sing Your praise.
Beautiful women, enchanting the mind in the celestial,
    terrestrial and nether worlds, sing Your praise.
Jewels that come from You, sites made sacred by You,
    sing Your praise.
Heroes and mighty warriors sing Your praise,
    the four sources of life sing Your praise,

Continents, constellations, and universes upheld by You
   sing Your praise.
Devotees who win Your affection, revelling in Your love,
   sing Your praise.
How many other singers and players I cannot conceive.
   Says Nanak, how then can I think of them?
That One, ever True Sovereign, true is the praise
   of that True One.
That One is, ever will be,
   and never will that Creator of the world not be.
Designer of this colourful diversity,
   Creator of this variegated world,
You watch over and sustain Your creation,
   all praise belongs to You.
Whatever You desire comes to pass,
   none can challenge Your commands.
Nanak says, You are the Sovereign of sovereigns,
   all abide by Your Will.

Asa Mahalla 1

1   Hearing of Your greatness, we stumble to speak of You,
   We could know Your measure, if only we could see You.
   Your greatness cannot be valued, cannot be expressed,
   Those who could speak of You remain absorbed in You.

   My great Sovereign, deep and unfathomable,
      You are an ocean of virtues.
   None can know how vast You are.

2   Sages amass their intuitions,
   Mathematicians amass their calculations,

Scholars, meditators and their leaders with their teachers,
But none can measure a grain of Your greatness.

3   All truth, all austerity and all good deeds,
     All holy miracles.
     No one achieves these powers without You.
     We are granted all things by Your ever-flowing grace.

4   How can a feeble one like me describe
     Your treasures brimming with virtues?
     What are our resources, but Your gifts?
     Nanak says, the True Enricher of all.

Asa Mahalla 1

1   I live to recite Your Name, if I did not, I should die,
     To recite the True Name is so hard.
     I hunger for the True Name;
     My hunger eats away all sorrow.

     My mother, how could I forget,
     The True Sovereign, whose Name is Truth?

2   To tell one grain of the True Name's greatness,
     Many have tried without gain.
     For all our praise altogether,
     The One is no greater, no less.

3   That One never dies, we'll have no cause for mourning.
     That One ever gives, our supplies are never ending.
     The virtue is this: there is no other,
     There never has been, nor will there ever be.

4 Great as You are, so too Your gifts,
  You created day for night to follow.
  Those who forget the Husband are the most lowly,
  Nanak says, without the Name, we are truly low-born.

Rag Gujri Mahalla 4

1 Devotees, True Guru, True Creator, I beseech You,
  Like worms we seek shelter in the True Guru,
  Have compassion, and grant us the radiance of the Name.

My Enlightening Friend, grant me the radiance
  of the divine Name.
The Name taught by the Guru is the breath of my life,
To praise the One is my daily custom.

2 Fortunate are the devotees, wrapped in faith, thirsty
   for the Divine.
  Hearing the Name, their thirst is quenched,
  Meeting with the faithful, their virtues sparkle.

3 They who do not taste the elixir of the Name
  Are unfortunate, they are with the god of death.
  They who do not seek the lap of the True Guru,
   nor the company of the pious, are accursed in this life,
   accursed in their life to come.

4 The foreheads of the devotees who seek the Truth Guru
   glow with fortune written from the dawn of time.
  Blessed, blessed is the true company
   in which the elixir is tasted.
  Nanak says, in such company, the Name is revealed.

Rag Gujri Mahalla 5

1   My mind, why this fretting and fussing,
        does the Divine not sustain you?
    Were beings not created among the rocks and mountains
        with their food laid out before?

Husband of the World, the truly faithful are liberated,
By the grace of the Guru, we win the highest station,
    Hearts, dry as wood, blossom lush green.

2   Our mothers who bore us, our fathers, neighbours,
        sons and wives — no one is anyone's support;
    The Creator cherishes each and every being;
        why then should you fear, my mind?

3   The crane flies high, travels hundreds of miles,
        leaving her young ones behind.
    Who feeds them? Who teaches them to peck?
        My mind, have you ever considered this?

4   The nine treasures and the eighteen powers are held
        in the palm of the Ruler's hand.
    Says Nanak the slave, I offer myself, again and again,
        I offer myself. Your limits cannot be encompassed.

Rag Asa Mahalla 4

1   The Divine Being is immaculate, the Purest of the pure.
        Unfathomable! Infinite!
    Everyone meditates, meditates on You,
        the True Creator of all.

All beings belong to You, You are their Provider.
Pious people, contemplate that One
    who dispels all suffering.
The Divine is Itself the Ruler, Itself the Servant.
    Nanak says, I am a mere mortal.

2   You are in every being, in all without distinction,
    the One Divine Being suffuses all.
Some are givers, some are beggars,
    this is part of Your enchanting sport.
You Yourself are the Giver, You Yourself are the Savourer.
    I know no one but You.
You are the Transcendent. Infinite! Totally infinite!
    Which of Your virtues could I describe?
They who serve You, who serve You,
    says Nanak the slave, I offer myself to them.

3   They who reflect, who reflect upon You,
    they live peacefully in this world.
They are freed, they are freed who remember the Divine,
    their snare of death is cut.
They who remember the Fearless One, the Fearless One,
    all their fears are dispelled.
They who serve, who serve my Beloved,
    they merge with the Divine Form.
Blessed, blessed are they who remember the Divine.
    Says Nanak the slave, I offer myself to them.

4   Infinite One, the treasures of devotion to You,
    of devotion to you, are overflowing and infinite.
Endless One, Your devotees, Your devotees praise you,
    countless are their adorations.
Infinite One, countless, countless are Your worshippers,

serving in penance and meditation.

My Infinite One, many, many are they who read scriptures
and perform rituals and ceremonies.

Says Nanak the slave, the devotees, the devotees
are they who please my Almighty.

5   You are the Primal Being, You are the transcendent Creator,
no one is as great as You.

Throughout the ages You alone exist.

Ever and ever, You are the Absolute One,
You are the immutable Creator.

Whatever You will, that comes to be.

Whatever You begin, that is accomplished.

You Yourself brought the universe into being,
You Yourself will dissolve it into nothingness.

Says Nanak the slave,
I sing praises of the Creator, the Knower of all.

Asa Mahalla 4

You are my true Creator, my beloved Husband.
Whatever pleases You will be,
    Whatever is mine has come from You.

1   All things are Yours, You are in everyone's mind.

They who receive Your favour
receive the Jewel of the Name.

They who face the Guru, profit;
they who face the ego, lose.

You separate us from You, and You unite us to You.

2   You are the ocean and all are within You,

Without You, there is no other.
All life is Your sport.
We separate from You, we unite with You;
    separated, our union is decreed by You.

3   Only by Your gift of knowledge do people know,
And they forever exalt and disclose Your virtues.
They who serve You find peace in their lives,
And they so easily merge with the divine Name.

4   You Yourself are the Creator, all that happens is Your doing,
Without You, there is no other.
Ever creating, You behold and know all.
Says Nanak the slave, through the Guru, You are revealed.

Asa Mahalla 1

1   Born into this lake of fiery waters
Their feet stuck in the slough of greed,
    I see them sinking.

My foolish mind, why don't you remember the One?
Forsaking the Divine, your virtues rot away.

2   Neither ascetic nor saint, nor learned,
    I am a fool, my life is spun in foolishness.
Says Nanak, this is my prayer,
    I seek the shelter of those who never forget You.

Asa Mahalla 5

1   You have obtained the human body,

Now is your chance to meet the Sustainer.
No other deed avails us,
But to join the faithful and recite the Name.

Let us prepare to swim across the ocean,
Life is waning in the dazzle of illusion.

2   Contemplation, penance, self-control, righteous action
       were of no benefit,
    I did not serve the faithful nor recognize
       the divine Sovereign.
    Says Nanak, our actions are low,
    Grant us goodness, we seek refuge in You.

Chaupai Benati

1   Give me Your hand and protect me,
    Fulfill the wishes of my heart.
    May my mind stay steadfast at Your feet,
    Care for me as Your own.

2   Destroy all my enemies,
    Save me with Your own hands.
    May my family live in peace,
    Creator, and all my devotees and Sikhs.

3   Protect me with Your own hands,
    Crush all my enemies today.
    May my wish come true,
    May I always thirst for worship of You.

4   May I contemplate no one but You,

Whatever I desire, may I receive from You.
Let my devotees and Sikhs cross the ocean,
Single out my enemies and slay them.

5 Protect me with Your own hands,
Absolve me from the fear of death,
Stay for ever on my side,
Revered One with the sword on Your banner, protect me.

6 Sustain me, my Sustainer,
My Beloved Sovereign, Friend of the pious,
Guardian of the poor, Destroyer of the corrupt.
You are the Owner of the fourteen worlds.

7 By Your command, Lord Brahma was born,
By Your command, Lord Shiva descended here,
By Your command, Lord Vishnu was revealed.
This entire universe is Your sport.

8 Who fashioned Lord Shiva as the ascetic,
Who crowned Lord Brahma as the king of the Vedas,
Who created and embellished the entire universe,
Our salutations to That One.

9 Who made the whole world,
Who produced gods, demons, and guardians,
Who is One from the beginning to the end of time,
Know That One as our Guru.

10 Our salutations are to That One alone,
Who creates all Its own citizens,
Who bestows virtue and happiness on the devoted,
Who instantly destroys all enemies.

11 You know the beatings of each and every heart,
   Recognize the pain of the good and the bad.
   From an ant to an elephant,
   You look upon all with favour and rejoice.

12 When the pious suffer, You suffer too
   When the pious rejoice, You rejoice too.
   You feel the pain of each and every being,
   Know the veils of each and every heart.

13 When You, Creator, expand,
   Your subjects take on their countless forms.
   When You recede,
   Their bodies merge with You.

14 The diverse bodies in this world,
   Praise You, each in their own way,
   But You remain apart without support
   The Vedas and the wise know Your mystery.

15 Formless! Immaculate! You need no support.
   Primal Being! Without colour, without time, without birth.
   Only a fool dares to describe
   The mystery that no scripture knows.

16 He confuses You with a stone,
   The great fool cannot distinguish the two.
   He calls Lord Shiva the Eternal One,
   He has no clue of the Formless One.

17 According to their own faculties,
   People describe You in so many ways.
   Your expanse cannot be fathomed;

We can never know how the world first began.

18 You have one form, without compare,
 Here You are a beggar, there You are a king.
 You created life from egg, from womb, from sweat,
 From earth, such riches are given.

19 Here You sit, sumptuous as a king,
 There You sit, shrunken as an ascetic;
 The whole creation displays wonders.
 You are before time, throughout time,
  and ever self-existent.

20 Grant me now Your protection,
 Defend my Sikhs, attack my foes.
 The tyrants who brutalize,
 Destroy them on the battlefield.

21 Those who seek Your lap, You who carry the banner,
 May their enemies die a terrible death.
 Those who bow at Your feet,
 May all their troubles be expelled.

22 Those who once remember the Timeless One,
 The time of death does not approach them;
 They are tended all the time,
 And in no time, their enemies are undone.

23 Those You look upon with favour,
 Their suffering ends at once,
 Their homes are filled with treasures, material and spiritual,
 Enemies cannot strike even their shadow.

24 Those who remember You once,
Are freed from the snare of death.
Those who say Your Name,
Are freed from poverty, enemy and misery.

25 You who have the sword on Your banner, I seek Your lap
Extend me Your hand and support me,
Guard me in every place,
Protect me from every enemy and misery.

Savayya

Since I held Your feet, I have eyes for no other.
Rama, Rahim, Purana or the Qur'an,
Countless faiths speak, but I do not follow any.
Smritis, Shastras and Vedas disclose many secrets,
but I do not believe any.
Revered One with the sword on Your banner,
all is fulfilled by Your favour. What can I say?
All I say is what You make me say.

Dohra

Rejecting all other doors, I have come to Yours.
Hold me in your arms, protect my honour,
Gobind is Your slave.

Ramkali Mahalla 3 Anand

1 My mother, I am in bliss, for I have found my True Guru,

The True Guru I found so easily,
     my mind rings with felicitations.
Jewel-like melodies with their families and fairies from afar
     have come to sing the Word within me.
Those with minds that house the Divine,
     they sing the sacred Word.
Nanak says, I am in bliss for I have found my True Guru.

2   My mind, stay for ever devoted to the Divine.
Devoted to the Divine, all your suffering is expelled,
You are welcomed, and all your actions fulfilled.
How could the all-Powerful Director slip from the mind?
Nanak says, my mind, stay for ever devoted to the Divine.

3   True Sovereign, what could Your home lack?
Your home overflows with everything,
     and all that we own has come from You.
Let us always sing Your glory, Your Name ever in mind.
Abiding with the Name, we resonate
     with the rapturous Word,
Nanak says, True Sovereign, what could Your home lack?

4   That True Name is my sole support, satisfying my hunger.
With peace and joy, It enters my mind,
     fulfilling all my desires.
I offer myself to the Guru who has bestowed
     all these glories.
Nanak says, listen to me, pious people, love the Word,
The True Name is my sole support.

5   The five instruments play the Word
     in that fortunate house of the self,
Fortunate is that body where Your power abides

and rings with the Word.
You have placed the five demons under their control,
    and You have slain thorny death.
Those graced by You from the beginning
    are devoted to the Name.
Nanak says, they are happy, and their house rings
    with the unstruck melody.

6   Fortunate ones, listen to this joyful song,
    all our wishes will be fulfilled,
We obtain the Transcendent, all grief and sorrow
    are left behind.
Suffering, sickness and fever depart,
    when we hear the Revelation.
Through the Guru, the pious win understanding,
    they are in bliss.
They who hear are pure, they who recite are pure,
    for they are suffused with the True Guru;
Nanak says, they who sit at the Guru's feet
    ring with the unstruck melody.

Mundavani Mahalla 5

In the platter, three things lie:
    truth, contentment, contemplation.
They contain the ambrosial Name,
    by which we are all sustained.
They who eat, they who savour,
    they are liberated.
This thing must not be abandoned;
    ever and ever, keep it in your heart.
The dark ocean can be crossed

if we take hold of the Guru's feet.
Says Nanak, this vastness is the Creator's handiwork.

Shalok Mahalla 5

I do not understand Your wonders,
nor the way You made me capable.
I am base, without virtue,
but You had compassion for me,
Compassion that showered me with boundless mercy,
and I found a friend in the True Guru.
Says Nanak, I live to hear the Name
that quickens body and mind with radiant joy.

Ardas

ARDAS ("Petition") is the basic prayer of the Sikhs which evolved as an anonymous composition within the community of the eighteenth century. It is recited while standing up. The leading member of the gathering, or any other person who is competent to read the Guru Granth, says the Ardas. The congregation joins in at intervals, exclaiming Vaheguru ("Wonderful Guru").

Ardas has powerful associations which remain constant for all occasions. These include remembering the Ultimate Reality, the Ten Gurus, their mergence with the Guru Granth, and events of Sikh heroism, devotion and martyrdom. Towards the end of the Ardas, a special blessing is called for the purpose of the gathering. Ardas finishes with the congregation praying for the prosperity and happiness of all humanity. While wishing for the good of all, the Sikhs bow in front of their sacred text, touch their foreheads to the ground, and seat themselves on the floor in front of it. Although not in the Guru Granth, Ardas is included in this selection because of its prominence in the life of the community.

There is One Being, all victory belongs to
  the Wonderful Guru,
May the divine Might help us.
The Tenth Guru's Ode to the divine Might.

First remember the divine Might,
  then think of Guru Nanak,
Next Gurus Angad, Amar Das and Ram Das,
  may they stand by us.
Gurus Arjan, Hargobind and Har Rai,
Think of Guru Harkrishan, that sight dispels all suffering.
Remember Guru Tegh Bahadur,
  who brings the nine treasures to our home.
May they support us everywhere.
May the Tenth Guru, Gobind Singh,
  support us everywhere.
The light of the Ten Gurus shines
  in the Guru Granth Sahib,
Consider its sacred word, envisage its sacred sight,
        And proclaim: *Vaheguru*, the Wonderful Guru!

The heroic deeds of the five beloved ones, the four princes,
  the forty who attained liberation,
The determined, the devout and the self-denying,
They who contemplated the Name, shared their earnings,
  established free kitchens, prepared for battle,
They who forgave others their faults,
Remember the purity and goodness of their deeds, Khalsaji,
        Proclaim: *Vaheguru*, the Wonderful Guru!

The Sikh men and women who gave their heads for
    their religion,
Whose limbs were cut off one by one,
Who were scalped, broken on the wheel, and sawn in pieces,
Who sacrificed their lives to serve the gurudwaras,
Their faith triumphed.
They served the Sikh religion with uncut hair to their
    last breath,
Remembering their steadfast faith, Khalsaji,
        Proclaim: *Vaheguru,* the Wonderful Guru!

Remember the five takhts, and all gurudwaras, Khalsaji,
        And proclaim: *Vaheguru,* the Wonderful Guru!

First of all, the Khalsa prays for remembrance of the
    Wonderful Guru, *Vaheguru, Vaheguru, Vaheguru!*
May this remembrance bring peace and happiness to all.
Wherever the Khalsa be, may Your protection and favour
    be there,
May our supplies in the kitchen and battlefield never fail,
May You uphold the honour of Your devotees,
May You grant victory to the Sikh community,
May the Sword aid us,
May the words of the Khalsa ever be exalted.
        Proclaim: *Vaheguru,* the Wonderful Guru!

Grant Your Sikhs the gift of the Sikh religion,
The gift of uncut hair, of good conduct and of knowledge,
The gift of trust, the gift of faith,
The gift of gifts, devotion to the Name,
And a bath in the sacred pool of Amritsar.
May the choirs that glorify You,
    the flags which herald You,

and the places where we learn of You endure for ever.
May righteous action ever triumph.

> Proclaim: *Vaheguru*, the Wonderful Guru!

May Sikhs lower their egos, and raise their wisdom,
You Yourself are the Sustainer of wisdom,

> *Vaheguru*, the Wonderful Guru!

Primal Being, eternal Sustainer of Your community,
May the Khalsa freely behold and serve Nankana Sahib
    and the other gurudwaras and all sacred places
From which we have been exiled.

Honour of the honourless, Power of the powerless,
    Shield of the shieldless,
Our true Parent, *Vaheguru*, the Wonderful Guru!
We humbly offer our prayers in Your presence.

[*At this point personal or communal prayers are said, eg.*]
May we be free of lust, anger, greed, attachment
    and pride.

Overlook our flaws in reading and reciting the sacred text.
May everyone's actions be fulfilled.
Join us with the faithful who inspire remembrance
    of Your Name.
Says Nanak, may Your Name be ever ascendant.
And, through Your Will,
    may everyone in the world fare well.

The Khalsa belongs to the Wonderful Guru,
Victory belongs to the Wonderful Guru!

Kirtan Sohila

KIRTAN SOHILA, "Hymn of Praise", is the finale to the evening prayers. It is recited just before going to bed as the Guru Granth is closed and ceremoniously carried to rest. It is also recited at cremation ceremonies. As with Rahiras, the hymns within Kirtan Sohila have a chorus which is placed in italics after the first stanza.

Kirtan Sohila consists of five hymns. The first three are by Guru Nanak, followed by one each from Guru Ram Das and Guru Arjan. The religious and artistic value of these hymns is superb. The first hymn visualizes the union of the individual self with the Ultimate Reality. The second presents the singularity of the Ultimate despite the endless diversity of scriptures, teachers and philosophies. The third rejects all modes of external piety and rituals, and vividly portrays the entire cosmos making a harmonious worship. Instead of salvers with lamps placed on them with incense and other offerings, the skies become an integrated platter, the sun and moon the lamps, stars the beads, and all vegetation an offering of flowers. Loud chanting is replaced by the inner unstruck melody playing motionlessly. The fourth hymn in the Sohila is by the Fourth Guru and it explains the import of the divine Name through which all suffering and transmigration is annulled. The fifth hymn, by Guru Arjan, celebrates life here in this world: we must avail ourselves of this wonderful opportunity to serve others and to win divine merit. The unknown Mystery becomes known to the enlightened person who thereafter enjoys the bliss and freedom of immortality. (Guru Granth, pp. 12-13.)

Sohila Rag Gauri Dipaki Mahalla 1

1   If there be a home for praise
       and thoughts of the Creator,
   Let that home sing in celebration
       and remember our Designer.

You sing a hymn of glory
   to my Fearless One,
I offer myself to the hymn of glory
   which brings everlasting joy.

2   Ever and ever, all creatures are nurtured
       and cared for by the Giver.
   Your bounty cannot be measured,
       who can reckon that Giver.

3   The wedding day is written,
       come friends, come pour the oil together.
   Give me your blessings, my friends,
       that I may join my Sovereign.

4   Each and every home receives this marriage thread,
       the invitations are sent to each and all.
   Nanak says, remember the Sender,
       for the day will come for all.

Rag Asa Mahalla 1

There are six schools with six leaders and six doctrines,
But there is only One Guru, though in countless guises.

My old friend, the school that sings the glory of our Creator,
Will bring you honour if you make it your home.

2 Moments become seconds, minutes, hours,
    days and months.
The sun is one, however many seasons there may be,
Nanak says, the Creator has so many forms.

Rag Dhanasri Mahalla 1

1 The sky is our platter, the sun and moon our lamps,
    it is studded with pearls, the starry galaxies,
The wafting scent of sandalwood is our incense,
    the gentle breeze, our whisk,
        all vegetation, the bouquet of flowers we offer to You.

What an act of worship!
This truly is Your worship, You who sunder life from death.
The unstruck sound within is the drum to which we chant.

2 You have a thousand eyes yet without eye are You,
You have a thousand faces yet without face are You,
You have a thousand feet yet without foot are You,
You have a thousand scents yet without scent are You,
    I am enchanted by Your wonders.

3 There is a Light in all, and that Light is You,

By that Light we are all illumined.
The Light is revealed through the Guru's teaching,
Whatever pleases You is worship of You.

4   My mind is greedy as the bumble-bee,
    Night and day I long to drink the ambrosia of
        Your lotus-feet.
    Nanak says, grant nectar to this thirsty bird,
    Grant me a dwelling in Your Name.

Rag Gauri Purbi Mahalla 4

1   This body is a city teeming with lust and anger.
        The company of holy people can shatter these vices.
    The meeting with the Guru that is written,
        anchors the mind to the immutable Centre.

There is merit in joining our palms to greet holy people,
There is merit in prostrating before holy people.

2   The deluded have not tasted the elixir of love,
        they are pierced by the thorn of ego.
    As they move on, the thorn pierces more painfully,
        till the end where death awaits with staff poised to strike.

3   But the devotees steeped in the Name
        are sundered from the suffering of life and death;
    They attain the Everlasting, the Supreme Being,
        and they are honoured in regions far and beyond.

4   We are poor and low, but we still belong to You,
        Highest of the high, protect us and keep us with You.

Nanak says, Your Name alone is my support and sustenance,
the Divine Name alone brings perfect joy.

Rag Gauri Purbi Mahalla 5

1   I beg you listen to me, my friends,
      now is the time to serve the holy ones,
   Divine profits earned here
      bring comfort in the hereafter.

   Our life grows shorter by the day.
   My mind, meet with the Guru and fulfill yourself.

2   This world is sunk in doubts and vices,
      but the enlightened can swim across.
   The one who is woken, the one who is given a sip of elixir,
      knows the story that cannot be told.

3   Make that transaction for which you came into this world,
      through the Guru, deposit the Divine in your mind.
   So easily will you find the joy that dwells
      within your own self,
      and no more will you enter the circle of living and dying.

4   Knower of all hearts, our Creator,
      Fulfiller of our desires,
   Your slave Nanak asks for this happiness,
      make me the dust of the feet of the holy ones.

Lavan

LAVAN, *composed by Guru Ram Das, is the hymn in four stanzas which is recited and sung to solemnize nuptials in Sikhism. The Sikh marriage ceremony is known as Anand Karaj, "Blissful Occasion"; it can take place anywhere, home or gurudwara, so long as the Guru Granth is present. This is the religious as well as the legal part of the marriage, and was officially recognized as such in India by the Sikh Marriage Act of 1909. The ceremony is now universally observed by the Sikhs.*

The marriage ceremony commences with the opening of the Guru Granth and with the reading of Lavan. Lavan, literally "circling", describes marriage as a rite of passage into higher and higher circles of existence. In Sikhism marriage is both literal and metaphorical. On the literal level it is a union of two people; on the metaphorical level it is a union of the microcosmic self with the Macrocosmic Reality. After husband and wife become one, they begin their passage together to a union with the Ultimate.

The journey begins with active work in the world and adoration of the Name. The second verse describes a higher state wherein the Ultimate Reality is recognized within all that is seen and heard. The Divine is encountered everywhere and the mystical melody is heard within the depths of the self. In the third circle, that feeling surges higher and the self becomes fully absorbed in the divine love. As the fourth round commences, the divine sweetness begins to pervade the entire self and unites the individual with the Infinite Self.

As each verse is recited and sung, the couple reverently circumambulate the Guru Granth clockwise. The relatives accompany them to show their support. During the fourth round, the bride and groom are showered with petals by the entire congregation as a sign of rejoicing. The ceremony concludes with the customary singing of passages from Anand (see pp. 136-8) and the recitation of Ardas (see pp. 141-5), with the entire congregation standing up this time. Finally hukam, the divine command, is received from the Guru Granth by opening it at random, and karahprashad, the sweet sacrament, is served to the entire congregation. (Guru Granth, pp. 773-4.)

1   Creator, as we revolve in the first divine circle,
         we resolve to return to the world of action.
     As we resolve to act rightfully, and make Your Word
         our god and scripture, our misdeeds are dispelled.
     Scriptures steadfastly urge us to act righteously
         and contemplate Your Name.
     By remembering the True Guru,
         all our misdeeds and offences are dispelled.
     Bliss is ours at once, we are blessed with great fortune,
         and the Divine tastes so very sweet.
     Nanak the slave says, in the first circle
         the wedding ceremony is begun.

2   In the second circle,
         we meet the True Guru, the Primal Being.
     By the fear of the Fearless One,
         our self gets rid of the filthy ego.
     In pure awe of the Divine, we sing praise day and night,
         and we see the Divine present everywhere.
     Infinite in all directions,
         intimate in everyone,
     Within and without, there is only the One.
         Joining the faithful, we sing songs of joy.
     Nanak the slave says, in the second circle
         the soundless Word begins to play.

3   In the third circle,

      the bliss of detachment fills the mind.

    By joining the faithful, we join the Transcendent One.

      We are blessed.

    We attain the Immaculate One, we worship the One

      with praise, and we recite the Word.

    By joining the faithful, we join the Blessed One.

      We tell the untellable story.

    Our heart begins to beat with the divine melody.

      We recite the Name with fortune glowing bright

      on our foreheads.

    Nanak the slave says, in the third circle

      the Divine One rises in our detached mind.

4   In the fourth circle,

      we find equanimity, we unite with the Divine One.

    Through the Guru, we naturally become one with the One,

      body and mind exult in delicious joy.

    But we taste the sweetness only if we please That One,

      by meditating day and night.

    My Guide, all my desires are fulfilled;

      through the divine Name, felicitations ring.

    The Sovereign's blessing completes the wedding rite;

      and the bride is in bliss with the Name in her heart.

    Nanak the slave says, in the fourth circle

      the imperishable Groom is wed.

COMMUNAL

Barah Maha

BARAH MAHA by Guru Nanak is in Rag Tukhari. It follows the seasonal cycle of the year. Many passages from it are popularly sung in Kirtan, the Sikh devotional concert. Barah Maha stands out in Sikh literature for its poetic splendour and philosophical importance. The movement of the twelve months — beginning with Chet, the first month of spring — and the effect of their passage on different species are vividly portrayed as metaphor for the phases of the spiritual journey. Guru Nanak richly fuses universal and particular time and space in the person of a young bride ardently searching for her divine Bridegroom through the cameos of the changing reality of the twelve months. (Guru Granth, pp. 1107-10.)

Tukhari Channt Mahalla 1

1   Hear us,
    we reap the fruits of our past deeds;
The joy or suffering each receives
    is good, for it comes from You.
This whole creation is Yours, what power have I?
    I cannot live one moment without the Divine.
Without the Lover I am friendless and in pain,
    but through the Guru, I drink the nectar.
We are enmeshed in the creation of the Formless One,
    yet to contemplate the Divine is the best of deeds.
Nanak says, the woman watches the way of her Lover.
    Hear me, You who pervade my very being.

2   The chatrik bird cries for the Lover,
    the koel bird sings in praise.
Embraced by her Beloved,
    the woman savours all delights.
Only she who pleases her Lover is embraced,
    and she alone is the true bride.
She makes her body with its nine doors the lofty palace,
    her own house enshrines the Beloved.
I am all Yours and You are mine, my Dearest,
    I revel in Your love night and day.
Nanak says, the chatrik cries, Beloved, Beloved,
    and the koel is made lovely by the call.

3   Hear me, my Belovèd, I am bathed in Your Love,
My mind and body are immersed in You,
    unable to forget You for an instant.
How can remembrance slip, I offer myself to You.
    I live only to sing Your praise.
No one belongs to me and I belong to no one;
    without the Divine One, I cannot live.
I seek Your support.
    By living at Your feet, my body is purified.
Nanak says, through the Guru's Word
    vision grows wide, comfort deep,
    and the mind is centred.

4   The ambrosial drops are showering down.
The Beloved comes to her so naturally,
    and the bride is so deeply in love.
The Divine One enters the bodily haven of the woman,
    awake and virtuous, who pleases her Groom.
In every home the Lover revels in the true brides;
    why then am I forsaken?
Clouds are cast low in the sky,
    and the showers are delightful,
    my mind and body are rapturous in love.
Nanak says, with the shower of the ambrosial Word
    the Divine One graciously enters our dwelling.

5   Chet is glorious, the bumble-bees delight in spring,
Barren woods bloom, and I long for my Beloved
    to come home.
If the Beloved does not come, how can a woman be happy?
    Her body trembles with yearning.
The koel sings happily in the mango grove;
    how can I bear the ache inside?

The bumble-bee hovers around the blossom boughs.
Mother, how can I live in this deathly state?
Nanak says, in the month of Chet, joy comes naturally,
if the woman finds the divine Groom in her house.

6 Vaisakh is glorious, the branches dressed
in their colourful best.
The woman watches at her door, for the divine Groom.
"Please have compassion and enter.
Come home, Beloved, take me across the impassable ocean;
without You I am not worth a penny.
Who could assess my worth if I were to please You?
Someone seek and show my Lover to me;
I know my Lover is within, not far away;
I recognize the Mansion of the Divine."
Nanak says, in the month of Vaisakh
one finds the Beloved if consciousness abides
in the Word, and mind is devoted in faith.

7 The month of Jeth is glorious, why forget the Beloved?
The land burns like an oven,
the woman offers her prayers.
Praying and reflecting on the Lover's virtues,
she seeks approval.
The Unattached One dwells in the True Mansion;
if That One allows, I will enter.
I am lowly and I am helpless; how can I attain
the joys of the Mansion without the Divine?
Nanak says, in Jeth, if the woman knows herself
in the One, she is graced with virtue.

8 Asarh is glorious, the sun blazes in the sky
And the earth suffers agony, scorching in heat like fire.

The sap is sucked dry in smouldering death for all,
    but the action continues;
The chariot of the sun moves on
    and the woman searches for shade.
    In the woods of the Bar, the cricket drones.
She who piles up misdeeds in this life faces suffering ahead
    but she who gathers truth receives everlasting joy.
Nanak says, those who are blessed with such a mind
    live and die steeped in the Divine.

9   In Savan, bloom, my mind, for the clouds have burst,
    and the monsoon season has arrived.
My mind and body yearn
    but my Lover is far away in foreign lands.
The Beloved does not come home, I am sighing to death,
    and the lightning strikes fear in me.
I lie alone on the bed, tormented;
    mother, the pain is like death to me.
Without the Divine One, how can there be sleep or hunger?
    What clothing can soothe the skin?
Nanak says, the bride is truly wed
    when she is embraced by her Beloved.

10   In Bhadon, she is lost in delusions,
    in her brimming youth, she is full of regret.
Water and land are awash
    in the roaring revelry of the season.
Rain sheeting the dark night,
    how can the young woman find joy?
    Frogs croak and peacocks screech,
The chatriks call for their beloved,
    and snakes go biting about.
The mosquitoes are stinging, the lakes overflowing,

but how can there be comfort without the Divine?
Nanak says, I will ask my Guru the way and go;
follow only that path which leads to the Lover.

11   In Assu, do come to me, my Beloved,
this woman is dying in agony.
She meets if the Beloved unites,
but not when she strays from the path.
Consumed by her misdeeds, she is abandoned,
her hair fades like the flowering water reeds.
More hot months ahead, the cold season behind me,
my heart trembles as I behold this passage.
In all directions, the boughs are green,
but that is sweet which ripens of its own accord.
Nanak says, come meet me, my Beloved, in Assu,
the True Guru has become my mediator.

12   In Kattak, we are bid to do what pleases You,
And the lamp lit with knowledge burns steadily.
As oil to the lamp, so the Beloved to the bride;
she brightens at their union.
False deeds end in false death;
virtuous deeds lead to liberation that ends death.
The devotees of the Name dwell in their true home,
holding You as the centre of all their hopes.
Nanak says, please open the door and meet me —
a single moment waiting seems like six months.

13   The month of Magghar is blessed,
divine virtues fill our hearts.
The worthy woman contemplates the virtues,
and seeks approval of the Immutable One.
The Creator is immutable, wise, the All-knowing,

while the world is all in flux.
Absorbed in knowledge and contemplation,
   we love only if it pleases the Lover.
Hearing songs, music and poetry in praise of the Name,
   all sorrow departs.
Nanak says, that wife is dear to the Husband
   who is utterly devoted in her love.

14   In Pokh, the frost comes, sapping life from woods and fields.
Why don't You come, You who dwell in my mind, body
   and on my tongue?
My mind and body are filled with the Life of the world,
   I revel in the Guru's Word.
Born of egg, foetus, sweat or earth,
   Your light radiates in all beings.
Grant me a glimpse, my compassionate Giver,
   grant me the wisdom to attain liberation.
Nanak says, the bride who is in love with her Groom,
   revels in the brilliance of the Reveller.

15   Magh is pure, the pilgrimage sites are found within.
Acquiring divine qualities, we naturally meet the Beloved.
Listen, my beautiful Groom, if I were to acquire Your virtues
   and please You — that would be my bath.
In the Ganga, in the Jamuna, their confluence
   with the Sarasvati, and in the seven seas —
   that would be my bath.
All charity, alms-giving and worship are in knowing
   that throughout the ages there is only One Being.
Nanak says, in Magh, we greatly rejoice
   in divine contemplation — that is our bath
   in the sixty-eight pilgrimage sites.

16   In Phalgun, the mind is enraptured by love,
Night and day it is in rapture, the self is lost.
If it please You, ego and greed are cast out.
    Grant me Your blessing and come home.
Without the Beloved I may adorn myself in many ways,
    but I will have no place in the Palace.
My necklaces, ribbons and silks adorn me,
    only when the Beloved seeks me.
Nanak says, when the Guru brought them together,
    the bride found the Groom within her own house.

17   The twelve months, seasons, dates, and days are all blessed.
Hours, minutes and seconds lead naturally
    to the True One.
Meeting the Beloved, all deeds are fulfilled,
    the Creator knows all procedures.
The One who adorns her is the One who loves her,
    and in that union she enjoys all delights.
When the Beloved embraces me,
    the nuptial bed within me is glorious.
    Through the Guru's Word, fortune brightens my forehead.
Nanak says, night and day the woman enjoys her Beloved;
    she is the eternally true bride of her divine Groom.

Shaloks of the Ninth Guru

THE SHALOKS ("Couplets") were composed by Guru Tegh Bahadur, the Ninth Guru, shortly before his execution in 1675. Brevity and simplicity constitute the poetic power of these fifty-seven couplets. They come at the end of the Guru Granth and are prominent in Bhog ("Pleasure") ceremonies. Bhog is a form of thanksgiving which concludes every reading of the Guru Granth. During Bhog, the congregation comes together and the reader begins to read slowly the last five pages of the Guru Granth beginning with the Shaloks and followed by Guru Arjan's Mundavani, the seal to the Guru Granth. (Guru Granth, pp. 1426-9.)

1   Unless we sing divine praise
        our life passes in vain;
    Says Nanak, love the Divine, my mind,
        as a fish loves water.

2   Why are we caught in worldly delights?
        Why can't we be free for a moment?
    Says Nanak, love the Divine, my mind;
        be saved from the snare of death.

3   Youth has passed away,
        old age taken over.
    Says Nanak, love the Divine, my mind;
        life hastens so quickly away.

4   Old age sets in,
        still we don't think of death.
    Says Nanak, fool,
        why don't you love the Almighty?

5   Riches, wives and all possessions
        we regard as our own.
    But which of them goes with us, my mind?
        Says Nanak, know that this is true.

6   Saviour of the fallen! Dispeller of fear!
        Home of the homeless!

Says Nanak, know That One
    abiding with us for ever.

7   Who gave us our body, who gave us wealth,
        That One we have not loved.
    Says Nanak, fool,
        why do you waver so wretchedly?

8   That One who blessed us with body and wealth,
        with comforts and beautiful homes.
    Says Nanak, listen my mind,
        why don't you remember That One?

9   The Bestower of all joys is the Divine,
        there is no other.
    Says Nanak, listen my mind,
        we are liberated by remembering That One.

10 Whose remembrance is liberating, my friend,
        love That One.
    Says Nanak, listen my mind,
        our life diminishes every moment.

11 Recognize, clever person,
        our body is made of the five elements.
    From That which it emerged, says Nanak,
        into That will it merge.

12 The Divine permeates each and every heart,
        so the faithful proclaim.
    Says Nanak, my mind remember That One
        who takes us across the world.

13   They who are free from joy and sorrow,
        from greed, passion and pride.
     Says Nanak, listen my mind,
        they indeed are the image of the Almighty.

14   They for whom praise and abuse are alike,
        for whom iron and gold are alike,
     Says Nanak, listen my mind,
        know that they are truly free.

15   They who are neither happy nor sad,
        who have neither friend nor foe,
     Says Nanak, listen my mind,
        they are truly free.

16   They who neither incite fear in others
        nor fear anyone themselves,
     Says Nanak, listen my mind,
        know that they are enlightened.

17   They who reject the poisons of the world
        and take up the way of detachment,
     Says Nanak, listen my mind,
        their foreheads glow with good fortune.

18   They who abandon fleeting delights and passions
        and are free from all attachments,
     Says Nanak, listen my mind,
        the Almighty abides in them.

19   They who abandon their own ego
        and recognize the Creator,
     Says Nanak, know this, my mind,

they truly are liberated!

20   The divine Name in this dark age
       dispels fear and ignorance.
     Says Nanak, they who recite It night and day,
       triumph in every action.

21   Recite divine praise with your tongues,
       hear the divine Name with your ears,
     Says Nanak, listen my mind,
       you will never succumb to death.

22   They who abandon attachment
       greed, passion, and pride,
     Says Nanak, they themselves are free
       and lead many others to freedom.

23   A dream or a show,
       know the world is so;
     Says Nanak, save for the Almighty,
       there is nothing real in here.

24   Lured by illusionary delights,
       we mortals waver night and day.
     Says Nanak, there is one in a million,
       who remembers the Divine.

25   Like a bubble on the waters
       ever rising and falling,
     Says Nanak, listen my friend,
       so is our world fashioned.

26   We are oblivious to all,

blinded by worldly intoxicants.
Says Nanak, without devotion
    we succumb to the snare of death.

27   If we want eternal happiness,
        we must ever seek the Lap of the Divine.
    Says Nanak, listen my mind,
        human life is hard to attain.

28   Ignorant fools
        chase fleeting delights;
    Says Nanak, without devotion,
        their life goes to waste.

29   The mortals who recite divine glory night and day,
        are the image of the Divine.
    Says Nanak, know this for sure,
        between the Divine and them, no difference lies.

30   Drowned in worldly delights,
        the mind forgets the Name.
    Says Nanak, without devotion to the Divine,
        what is the purpose of life?

31   We do not remember the Divine,
        through the stupor of wordly intoxicants.
    Says Nanak, without devotion
        we succumb to the snare of death.

32   In times of joy, there are countless friends;
        in times of sorrow, not one.
    Says Nanak, my mind, be devoted.
        That One is our friend for ever.

33 For so long have I wandered from birth to birth,
    and still have not conquered my fear of death.
  Says Nanak, my mind, be devoted;
    so will you dwell with the Fearless One.

34 I have tried so hard
    but cannot give up my ego.
  Says Nanak, I am caught in ignorance;
    save me, Almighty One!

35 Life has three stages:
    Childhood, youth and old age.
  Says Nanak, without devotion
    they come to naught.

36 Sunk in avarice, we left undone
    all that was to be done.
  Says Nanak, time has passed,
    ignorant fool, why weep now?

37 The mind is sunk in wordly delights,
    It cannot be freed, my friend,
  Says Nanak, like a fresco
    which cannot be pared from its wall.

38 We hope for something
    while quite another happens.
  Says Nanak, while we busily deceive others
    our own minds are ensnared by death.

39 We strive for comforts
    but never for pain.
  Says Nanak, listen my mind,
    all happens as the Divine wills.

40 The world goes begging around,
    but the sole bestower is the Divine.
  Says Nanak, my mind, contemplate That;
    so will all your works be fulfilled.

41 Why all this false pride?
    The world is but a dream.
  Says Nanak, my mind,
    none of it belongs to you.

42 This body in which we take such pride,
    vanishes in an instant, my friend.
  Says Nanak, they who exalt the Divine,
    they conquer the world.

43 They who enshrine the Divine in their self,
    know them as liberated.
  Says Nanak, know this for sure,
    between the Divine and them, no difference lies.

44 They who are devoid
    of devotion for the One,
  Says Nanak, know them to be
    pigs and dogs.

45 Like the faithful dog
    that never leaves its owner's house,
  Says Nanak, worship the Divine,
    with single mind.

46 Pilgrimage, fasts and charity;
    while there is pride in the heart,
  Says Nanak, all such actions are as futile

as an elephant's bath.

47   The head shakes, feet falter,
        eyes lose their light.
     Says Nanak, knowing this to be our end,
        why aren't we suffused with the divine nectar?

48   I saw the world as my own,
        but nothing here belongs to anyone.
     Says Nanak, devotion alone is constant;
        keep this in mind.

49   The world is false;
        know this, my friend.
     Says Nanak, it crumbles
        like a wall of sand.

50   Rama departed, Ravana departed,
        so did their huge families.
     Says Nanak, nothing here abides;
        the world is but a dream.

51   We should worry only
        about what we can prevent.
     Says Nanak, this is the way;
        everything is passing.

52   What is born must die,
        if not today then tomorrow.
     Says Nanak, let us sing divine praise
        and free ourselves from all fetters.

53   I am weakened and shackled,

no effort avails.
Says Nanak, protect me
as once You helped the elephant.

54   I am empowered and unshackled;
all my efforts are fulfilled.
Says Nanak, all is in Your hands;
You are our constant companion.

55   Friends and relatives desert,
none is our ally for ever.
Says Nanak, in times of distress
You are our only shelter.

56   The Name is eternal, the faithful are eternal,
eternal is the sustaining Guru.
Says Nanak, there are few in this world
who remember the Guru's Word.

57   Let us enshrine the Name in our hearts,
for none is its equal.
The Name dispels our suffering;
the Name brings us the sight of You.

PERSONAL AND COMMUNAL

Sukhmani

SUKHMANI is Guru Arjan's composition in Rag Gauri. Sukh means "peace" and mani is both "pearl" and "mind", so the title can be translated as "Pearl of Peace" or "Mind of Peace". Sikh tradition maintains that Guru Arjan composed it under the beri tree which is still beside the sacred pool of Ramsar in Amritsar.

Sukhmani runs to almost 2,000 lines and is divided into twenty-four sections. Each section contains eight stanzas (ashtpadi), prefaced by a couplet (shalok) which embodies the central theme. The exception is an additional couplet after the first stanza which introduces the title of the hymn. The Pearl of Peace is described as the ambrosial Name, cherished by the devout in their selves. The entire hymn extols the importance of the Name.

Although it is not part of the daily routine, Sukhmani is very popular and many Sikhs recite it daily. During the summer, around the time of the anniversary of Guru Arjan's martyrdom, many men and women gather in homes or gurudwaras to read it together. Several copies of the Sukhmani are made available for the congregation. Someone begins to read out a section, and any one who wishes may join at the end to lead in the reading of the next section. The couplets are read by the entire group. This joint reading of lyrical poetry brings peace to the reader and the listener alike. (Guru Granth, pp. 262-96.)

1   *My homage to the primal Guru, my homage to the Guru*
        who has existed throughout the ages.
    My homage to the true Guru,
        my homage to the supreme Guru

1   Remember, Remember the One whose remembrance
        brings peace
    And dispels pain and sorrow from the body.
    Remember the One who alone upholds the universe,
    Whose Name is contemplated by millions.
    The auspicious words of all Vedas, Puranas and Smriris
    Arise from the single Word of the divine Name.
    They who possess even one jot of Your Name
    Are great beyond telling.
    They who yearn only for a vision of You,
    Says Nanak, I seek liberation in their company.

    The ambrosial Name is the pearl of peace,
    The faithful cherish it deep in their selves.

2   Contemplating the Divine, we do not return to the womb,
    Contemplating the Divine, the god of death vanishes,
    Contemplating the Divine, death itself abstains,
    Contemplating the Divine, enemies flee,
    Contemplating the Divine, all obstacles give way,
    Contemplating the Divine, we stay alert day and night,
    Contemplating the Divine, fear is cast off,

Contemplating the Divine, we escape suffering.
Contemplate the Divine in the company of the faithful.
Says Nanak, all treasures lie in the divine Radiance.

3   Contemplating the Divine, we gain power of body, spirit
         and matter,
     Contemplating the Divine, we acquire knowledge,
         concentration and the essence of wisdom,
     Contemplating the Divine, we win the merit of meditation,
         penance and worship,
     Contemplating the Divine, duality is dissolved,
     Contemplating the Divine, we bathe in sacred places,
     Contemplating the Divine, we are honoured in the Court,
     Contemplating the Divine, we act for the good,
     Contemplating the Divine, we blossom and bear fruit,
     But they alone contemplate who are divinely inspired,
     Says Nanak, I embrace their feet.

4   Divine contemplation is the highest deed,
     Divine contemplation liberates multitudes,
     Divine contemplation quenches our thirst,
     Divine contemplation deciphers all things,
     Divine contemplation dispels fear of death,
     Divine contemplation fulfills our hopes,
     Divine contemplation purifies our mind.
     Thus does the ambrosial Name resonate in the heart.
     The Divine dwells on the tongue of the faithful.
     Says Nanak, I enslave myself to those who serve You.

5   Those who contemplate the Divine are wealthy,
     Those who contemplate the Divine are respected,
     Those who contemplate the Divine are admired,
     Those who contemplate the Divine are true leaders,

Those who contemplate the Divine are totally free,
Those who contemplate the Divine are rulers of all,
Those who contemplate the Divine abide in bliss,
Those who contemplate the Divine are ever invincible.
Only they who receive divine compassion begin
    to contemplate.
Says Nanak, I seek the dust of their feet.

6   Those who contemplate the Divine are kind and charitable,
Those who contemplate the Divine, I offer myself to them,
Those who contemplate the Divine have beautiful faces,
Those who contemplate the Divine enjoy
    comfortable lives,
Those who contemplate the Divine conquer their egos,
Those who contemplate the Divine live morally,
Those who contemplate the Divine have countless joys,
Those who contemplate the Divine live close to the One.
Through the grace of the faithful, we remain alert
    day and night.
Says Nanak, contemplation is the lot of the fortunate.

7   Contemplating the Divine, all tasks are fulfilled,
Contemplating the Divine, we are never embittered,
Contemplating the Divine, our words are praise,
Contemplating the Divine, we are at peace,
Contemplating the Divine, we approach the
    immutable Seat,
Contemplating the Divine, the heart blossoms,
Contemplating the Divine, the wondrous melody is heard.
Infinite is the peace of divine contemplation.
Only they who receive divine favour contemplate.
Says Nanak, I seek their refuge.

8   Through Divine contemplation, our devotion is revealed,
Through Divine contemplation, the Vedas were inspired,
Through Divine contemplation, many become saintly, ascetic
    and compassionate,
Through Divine contemplation, the lowly win fame in all
    four directions,
Through Divine contemplation, the entire earth was
    established,
Contemplate, contemplate the Divine, the Cause
    of all causes,
Through Divine contemplation, all visible forms are seen,
In Divine contemplation, the Formless One exists.
They who are divinely enlightened,
Says Nanak, through the Guru they alone receive
    the gift of contemplation.

2   *You are the dispeller of the pain and suffering of the poor.*
    You pervade each and every heart,
    Protector of the unprotected.
    I have come to seek Your shelter, says Nanak,
    stand by my side.

1   Where there is no mother, father, son, friend, or brother,
There, my mind, the Name is our only aid.
When the fearful ambassadors of Death oppress us,
Then the Name will be our only ally.
When we are caught in grievous troubles,
At once the Name frees us.
Where endless atonements do not save us,
The Name dispels our countless misdeeds.
My mind, meditate upon the Name;
Says Nanak, so do we find boundless joy.

2   Conquering the world, the conqueror still suffers;
Contemplating the Name alone brings joy.
Piling up millions, the river of desire flows on and on;
Contemplating the Name alone takes us
    to the shore of freedom.
The countless pleasures of the visible world
    do not quench our thirst;
Contemplation of the Name alone brings satisfaction.
On the path to death we walk by ourselves;
Contemplation of the Name is our sole companion
    and comfort.
May we always contemplate the Name.
Says Nanak, by the grace of the Guru we attain supreme
    bliss.

3   A million arms may come to our rescue,
But only contemplation of the Name can save us.
When countless troubles strike us,
At once, the Name frees us.
Caught in the wheel of endless births and deaths,
We find lasting peace by contemplating the Name.
The filth of ego is hard to cleanse,
But a million faults are washed away by contemplating
    the Name
My mind, contemplate this Name with radiant love,
Says Nanak, contemplate in the company of the faithful.

4   As we journey along the endless road,
The Name is our wholesome fare.
As we journey blind along a dark path
The Name is our shining light.
On a journey where no one knows us,
The Name is our distinctive crest.

On a dreadful journey in searing heat,
The Name is our refreshing shade.
On a journey where thirsty desires tug at us,
Says Nanak, the life-giving ambrosial Name showers
    down upon us.

5   The daily round of the faithful turns on the Name,
The Name dwells in the mind of the holy ones,
The Name is the refuge of the devotees,
Countless people are liberated by the Name,
Day and night, the holy ones sing praise of the Divine.
The Name is their medicine for all ills,
The Name is a treasure for those
Who are blessed by the Transcendent.
Their minds and bodies shine with the bright colours
    of the One,
Says Nanak, they are truly wise and discerning.

6   The Name is our path to liberation,
The Name is our wholesome fare,
The Name is our beauty and charm.
With the Name, we are never blocked.
The Name is our honour,
The Name brings us glory,
The Name is our joy and union.
With the Name, we feel no alienation.
The devotees are dyed deep in service to the Name,
Says Nanak, I worship the Ultimate.

7   The Divine is the wealth and treasure of the devotees,
By the One they are blessed with the sacred Treasure.
The Divine One is the mighty support of the devotees,
They recognize no other besides the Light,

Every thread of their being is drenched in love.
Drunk with the Name, they are wrapped in silence,
Day and night they meditate upon the Name.
They are known throughout the world, their fame cannot
    be concealed.
Contemplation liberates countless devotees,
Says Nanak, and they liberate so many more.

8   The Name is the celestial tree, Its fruit fulfils our hunger,
The Name is the celestial cow, Its milk quenches our thirst.
Sacred discourse is the greatest joy,
Hearing the Name, pain and suffering end.
The glory of the Name resonates in the heart of the faithful,
When the faithful are inspired, all misdeeds flee.
To join the company of the faithful is a great blessing,
By serving the faithful, we remember the Name.
The Name has no equal,
Says Nanak, few are they who attain It.

3   *There are so many sacred texts and I have searched them all.*
But they do not reach the Name, says Nanak,
    that is priceless above all.

1   Practise meditation, austerity, knowledge and concentration,
Discuss all six philosophies and countless sacred texts,
Perform yoga and various rituals,
Renounce the world and wander in the forest;
Whatever we may do —
Give charity to the poor, and rich butter to the god of fire,
Cut the body into pieces, offer them in a holocaust,
Observe all kinds of fasts and vows —
None comes close to contemplation of the Name.

Says Nanak, through the Guru's guidance,
    meditate upon the Name just once.

2   Were we to roam the nine continents, and live
        the longest life,
    Were we to renounce the world and become
        the greatest ascetic,
    Were we to offer our body to the fire,
    Were we to give away gold, thoroughbred horses
        and lands in charity,
    Were we to perform purification and yoga,
    Were we to take up the strict disciplines of the Jain way,
    Were we to have our body cut in tiny pieces,
    Even then the filth of ego would not go.
    There is nothing that equals the Name,
    Says Nanak, through the Guru's guidance,
        contemplation of the Name emancipates us.

3   We may die at our chosen holy place,
    But pride and ego do not die.
    We may cleanse ourselves day and night,
    But the filth of the mind is never cleansed.
    Our body may practise great discipline,
    But the deadly desires do not leave our mind.
    We may bathe our mortal body to excess,
    But can that wall of mud ever be cleansed?
    My mind, the glory of the Name is supreme,
    Says Nanak, through the Name,
        many evildoers have been redeemed.

4   Clever deeds will not erase the fear of death,
    Countless acts will not allay our thirst,
    Different clothes will not douse the fire of desire,

Countless devices will not admit us to the Court.
Whether we fly into the sky or sink into the underworld,
    we will not escape,
We are ensnared in the net of attachment cast by the
    visible world.
The god of death punishes all other actions
And accepts nothing but remembrance of the Name.
By contemplating the Name suffering departs;
Thus do I speak spontaneously, says Nanak.

5   If we want to achieve the four goals of life,
We must serve the faithful.
If we want to end our suffering,
We must always recite the Name in our heart.
If we want honour for ourselves,
We must abandon our ego and join the company
    of the faithful.
If we fear the cycle of life and death,
We must seek refuge with the faithful.
They who long to envisage the One
Says Nanak, I offer myself to them.

6   That person is supreme
Who has overcome ego in the company of the faithful.
Such a one whose self-regard is the lowest
Truly should be reckoned as the highest.
This one, as humble as the dust on everyone's feet,
Discerns the presence of the Name in every heartbeat.
This one whose mind is wiped clean of evil
Knows all creation as a good friend.
Such a person views suffering and joy alike.
Says Nanak, such a one transcends good and evil.

7   For the destitute, Your Name is wealth,
For the homeless, Your Name is home,
For the lowly, Your Name is honour,
You grant Your gifts to every heart.
Creator of all and Cause of all causes,
You understand our deepest thoughts,
You alone can grasp Your vastness,
You are suffused in Your own radiance,
You alone can fully praise Yourself,
Says Nanak, no other can fathom You.

8   The best faith of all faiths
Is to contemplate the Name and live in purity.
The supreme ritual of all rituals
Is to dispel ill-will in the company of the faithful.
The cardinal venture of all ventures
Is to meditate constantly on the Name.
The immortal language of all languages
Is to hear and recite the Divine glory.
The best place of all places
Is the body where dwells the Name, says Nanak.

4   *My ignorant and worthless self, always remember the One.*
Remember the one who created you, says Nanak,
    only the One will stand by you till the end.

1   Let us recall the wondrous gifts of the all-pervading One,
Who brings us from seed to this beautiful form,
Who sculpts and embellishes us perfectly,
Who protects us in the heat of the womb,
Who nourishes us with milk in our childhood,
Who feeds us treats and pleasures in our brimming youth,

Who draws our kin near to care for us in old age,
Who provides for us in our bed at the very end,
We worthless ones do not see the divine virtues,
Says Nanak, our life only succeeds with Your blessing.

2   By Whose blessing we live comfortably on earth
And rejoice with our children, relatives, friends and wives,
By Whose blessing we drink cool water
And enjoy the priceless comforts of air and fire,
By Whose blessing we revel in all joys,
And dwell in the midst of this vast panorama,
By Whose blessing we receive hands, feet, ears, eyes
    and tongue,
That One we abandon and attend to another.
Such is the sorry state of the ignorant and the blind.
Says Nanak, rescue us Yourself, Infinite One.

3   The One supports us from beginning to end,
The fool does not love That One.
Service of the One wins us the nine treasures,
The dupe is not attracted to That One.
The Sovereign is always present at our side,
The blind imagines That One is far away.
Serving the One brings glory in the hereafter,
The ignorant fool ignores That One.
We are always forgetful and mistaken.
Says Nanak, save us, our infinite Saviour.

4   We discard the Jewel, and busy ourselves with shells,
We discard the Truth, and consume ourselves with lies.
What is ephemeral, we clutch as eternal,
What is inevitable, we carelessly dismiss,
What is in flux, we ardently clasp.

Our everlasting Companion, we rashly forsake.
We wash away the sandalwood fragrance,
And like an ass, roll blithely in dust.
We have fallen into the dreadful well of ignorance,
Says Nanak, Compassionate One, lift us up.

5   Our caste is human but our deeds are bestial,
Day and night we spend in deceit.
Outside we are pious, inside we seethe with profanity,
We cannot hide however much we try.
We display scholarship, discipline and purity,
We conceal greed's barking dog inside.
The fire of lust burns within, penitential ashes
    clothe our body.
With stones tied around our neck, how can we
    swim across the ocean?
Those in whom the One dwells,
Says Nanak, they are wrapped in serenity.

6   How are the blind to find their way by hearing?
Led by the hand, they reach their destination.
How can the deaf solve riddles?
What we call night, they think of as day.
How can the mute sing songs of devotion?
When they try, the tune is lost.
How can the disabled build houses on mountains?
They cannot ascend those heights.
Our compassionate Creator, we make our prayer to You,
Says Nanak, we are liberated only by Your favour.

7   We have forgotten our everlasting Friend,
And fallen in love with the enemy.
We dwell in a house of sand,

Absorbed in the games of the visible world.
We firmly believe in fleeting illusions,
The thought of death never occurs to our ignorant self.
In enmity, hate, lust, anger, attachment,
In lies, misdeeds, greed and deceit,
Ensnared in these, we have migrated from life to life.
Says Nanak, in Your benevolence — save us.

8   You are our Sovereign, to You we pray.
Our body and life are Your gifts.
You are our Mother, You are our Father,
   and we are Your children.
Your grace is the source of our countless joys.
No one knows Your extent,
Higher than the Highest is our Creator.
All existence is perfectly beaded on Your thread,
All that happens is by Your Will.
Your reality, Your dimensions, You alone know,
Says Nanak the slave, I offer myself ever to You.

5   *Abandoning the gracious Giver, we addict ourselves to other*
delights and never succeed.
Says Nanak, without the Name, we lose all honour.

1   The ten gifts we receive, we quickly forget,
For one that we miss we lose our faith.
What if That One gave us nothing?
   What if the ten gifts were taken back?
Then what would we do?
Helpless before our Sovereign,
We must always pay homage.
Those who are drawn to the divine sweetness,

Are full of joy and peace.
Those who are blessed to live by the Will,
Says Nanak, they win all the treasures of the world.

2   Our Merchant dispenses untold wealth;
We spend it on food, drink, fun and games.
But if the Merchant recalls part of the deposit,
Our ignorant mind begins to protest.
Thus we lose our credit
And never regain our trust.
All things we must offer to Whom they belong,
We must bow low to the Will.
So will we be blessed four times over,
Says Nanak, the Sovereign is always generous.

3   There are countless attractions in the visible world,
Surely we should see their transience.
If we attach ourselves to the shade of the tree,
We will mourn its passing.
Whatever we see is fleeting,
Why then are we blindly entangled?
If we fall in love with an itinerant,
We will be left with no body to embrace.
My mind, the love of the Name brings peace,
Says Nanak, You Yourself so graciously inspire it in us.

4   Our body, wealth, family — all are fleeting.
Fleeting are ego, attachment, and every visible thing,
Fleeting are power and youth, property and riches,
Fleeting are the dreadful passions of lust and anger,
Fleeting are chariots, elephants, horses, and regalia,
Fleeting is the laughter of our illusory pleasures,
Fleeting are deceit, desire and arrogance,

Fleeting is pride in our self.
Only devotion in the company of the faithful is everlasting.
Says Nanak, I live to worship the divine Feet.

5   False are the ears which hear slander against others,
False are the hands which snatch the wealth of others,
False are the eyes which crave the beauty of another's wife,
False is the tongue which savours tastes other than the One,
False are the feet which run to harm others,
False is the mind which hankers after the goods of others,
False is the body which does not help others,
False is the nose which inhales illicit smells.
Without true understanding, we stray in lies,
Says Nanak, that body alone is worthy which remembers
    the Name.

6   Worthless in life is worship of the body,
How can we be pure without the Truth?
Without the Name, the body is worthless and blind,
And life leaves a bad taste in the mouth.
Without contemplation, days and nights are worthless
    and wasted,
As crops without rain.
Without recitation of the Name all deeds are worthless,
As money hoarded by a miser.
Blessed are they who resonate with the Name,
Says Nanak, I ecstatically offer myself to them.

7   We display discipline but our deeds are quite different,
We talk of spiritual union but have no love in our hearts.
The All-knowing who sees through everything
Is not fooled by our façade.
We preach but we do not practise

As we come and go in the cycle of birth and death.
Those who have the Formless One within
Redeem the whole world through their teaching.
Those who please You come to recognize You,
Says Nanak, I pay homage at their feet.

8   We offer our prayers, but the Sovereign knows all before.
How You celebrate Your own creation!
You Yourself decide how we fare.
Some think of You as far away, some feel You close by.
You transcend all skills and cleverness,
You truly know our inmost selves.
They who please You, You draw towards You.
How You permeate each and every place.
Those You bless, they alone become Your devotees,
Says Nanak, remember the Divine every moment.

6   *Lust, anger, greed, attachment, and pride,*
      may they all leave me.
    Says Nanak, I have come to Your refuge,
      grant me Your blessing, my supreme Guru.

1   Through whose bounty we taste the six and thirty delicacies,
We must keep That One in our mind.
Through whose bounty we perfume our body,
By remembering That One we reach the highest state.
Through whose bounty we live happily in our homes,
We must always celebrate That One in ourselves.
Through whose bounty we enjoy our family,
We must meditate upon That One night and day.
Through whose bounty we revel in pleasure,
Says Nanak, remember That One ever worthy of
remembrance.

2   Through whose bounty we wear lovely silks,
Why abandon That One and desire another?
Through whose bounty we sleep in comfort,
We should exalt That One night and day.
Through whose bounty we are honoured by all,
We should recite aloud the glory of That One.
Through whose bounty we perform our duty,
We should always remember that single Supreme Being.
Contemplating the Beloved we are exalted in the Court,
Says Nanak, with honour we enter our true Home.

3   Through whose bounty we received this
      healthy golden body,
We must attach ourselves with love to That One.
Through whose bounty our honour is maintained,
Our mind finds peace by venerating That One.
Through whose bounty all our faults are hidden,
We should seek refuge in That One.
Through whose bounty we succumb to no enemy,
We should remember that Exalted One with every breath.
Through whose bounty we received this precious body,
Says Nanak, we should be totally devoted to That One.

4   Through Whose bounty we wear jewels,
Why are we too lazy to remember That One?
Through Whose bounty we ride horses and elephants,
My mind, never forget That One.
Through whose bounty we own property and gardens,
We should keep That One beaded like pearls in our mind.
Through whose bounty our minds and bodies are shaped,
Sitting or standing, we must ever remember That One.
Contemplate That One, the only Unfathomable One,
Says Nanak, That One protects us here and in the hereafter.

5   Through whose bounty we give alms and charity,
We must remember That One day and night.
Through whose bounty we conduct our duties and
    obligations,
We must remember That One with every breath.
Through whose bounty we receive our beautiful form,
We must always remember That One's incomparable beauty.
Through whose bounty we receive our noble birth,
We must always remember That One day and night.
Through whose bounty we are honoured,
Says Nanak, through the Guru's blessing,
    we exalt That One.

6   Through whose bounty our ears hear the sacred melody,
Through whose bounty our eyes behold the sublime wonder,
Through whose bounty our tongue recites the ambrosial
    Word,
Through whose bounty we live in peaceful harmony,
Through whose bounty our hands perform good deeds,
Through whose bounty we blossom into perfection,
Through whose bounty we reach the highest state,
Through whose bounty we find peace and equanimity,
Why discard That One and desire another?
Says Nanak, through the Guru's blessing, may our minds
    be enlightened.

7   Through whose bounty we are acclaimed in the world,
My mind, never forget That One.
Through whose bounty we are exalted in the world,
My foolish mind, why do you not worship That One?
Through whose bounty our tasks are fulfilled,
My mind, know That One as always present.
Through whose bounty we find Truth,

My mind, enshrine That One.
Through whose bounty we are all liberated,
Says Nanak, contemplate That One.

8   Touched by You, they contemplate Your Name,
Inspired by You, they sing Your praise.
By Your favour, we are enlightened,
By Your compassion, our hearts blossom like the lotus.
When You are pleased, You dwell in our minds.
By Your compassion, our wisdom is heightened.
In Your benevolence, all treasures are contained.
None of us accomplishes anything on our own.
Sustainer, as You impel us, so we go,
Says Nanak, there is nothing our own hands can hold.

7   *Unfathomable, Infinite is the Transcendent One, they who*
        speak of That One are liberated.
    Says Nanak, listen, I beg you my friend, to the marvellous story
        of the faithful.

1   In the company of the faithful, our faces glow,
In the company of the faithful, our impurities wash away,
In the company of the faithful, pride disappears,
In the company of the faithful, wisdom appears,
In the company of the faithful, we see the One close by,
In the company of the faithful, our conflicts flee,
In the company of the faithful, we receive the Jewel of
    the Name,
In the company of the faithful, we concentrate on attaining
    the One,
Who can truly honour the faithful?
Says Nanak, the praise of the faithful partakes of the Divine.

2   In the company of the faithful,
       the Imperceptible is perceived,
    In the company of the faithful, life always bears fruit,
    In the company of the faithful, the five passions are under
       control,
    In the company of the faithful, we taste the immortal elixir,
    In the company of the faithful, we are humble
       as the dust of everyone's feet,
    In the company of the faithful, our speech
       becomes eloquent,
    In the company of the faithful, we stop chasing to and fro,
    In the company of the faithful, we acquire serenity,
    In the company of the faithful, we are not enticed by the
       visible world,
    Says Nanak, when we join the faithful, the Divine is pleased.

3   In the company of the faithful, the enemy becomes
       our friend,
    In the company of the faithful, we are cleansed of all filth,
    In the company of the faithful, we are freed of enmity,
    In the company of the faithful, we do not go astray,
    In the company of the faithful, no fellow being seems bad,
    In the company of the faithful, we know supreme bliss,
    In the company of the faithful, we are freed of all suffering,
    In the company of the faithful, we are rid of our ego,
    You Yourself know the greatness of the faithful,
    Says Nanak, the faithful and the Divine unite in friendship.

4   In the company of the faithful, we do not run in circles,
    In the company of the faithful, we find peace,
    In the company of the faithful, we fathom the Unfathomable,
    In the company of the faithful, we bear the unbearable,
    In the company of the faithful, we live in an exalted state,

In the company of the faithful, we reach the Mansion,
In the company of the faithful, we resolve to act righteously,
In the company of the faithful, we experience only the
    Transcendent,
In the company of the faithful, we find the treasure of the
    Name,
Says Nanak, I offer myself to the faithful.

5   In the company of the faithful, we liberate our people,
In the company of the faithful, we save our companions,
    friends and families,
In the company of the faithful, we obtain that treasure
Which profits everyone.
In the company of the faithful, the god of death is our
    servant,
In the company of the faithful, we are honoured by the gods,
In the company of the faithful, evil is dispelled,
In the company of the faithful, we sing immortal praise,
In the company of the faithful, we reach our destination,
Says Nanak, in the company of the faithful, our life is
    rewarding.

6   In the company of the faithful, we cease to struggle,
By their very sight we are redeemed,
In the company of the faithful, misdeeds are dispelled,
In the company of the faithful, hell is banished,
In the company of the faithful, peace is found
    here and in the hereafter,
In the company of the faithful, we are united with the One
    we lost.
Whatever we desire, we are granted,
In the company of the faithful, we are not
    left empty-handed.

The Transcendent abides in the heart of the faithful.
Says Nanak, we are liberated by hearing the joy of the
faithful.

7   In the company of the faithful, hear the Name,
In the company of the faithful, recite the praise,
In the company of the faithful, we are ever mindful,
In the company of the faithful, we are surely liberated,
In the company of the faithful, we taste the sweetness of the
Divine,
In the company of the faithful, we see the One in each and
every heart,
In the company of the faithful, we obey the Will,
In the company of the faithful, we are delivered for eternity,
In the company of the faithful, we are freed from all sickness,
Says Nanak, we are fortunate to meet with the faithful.

8   The greatness of the faithful is beyond ancient scriptures,
For these record only what they have heard.
The praise of the faithful is beyond the three strands,
The praise of the faithful extends everywhere.
The glory of the faithful has no limit,
The glory of the faithful is forever infinite,
The glory of the faithful is the highest of the high,
The glory of the faithful is the greatest of the great,
The glory of the faithful can be voiced by the faithful alone,
Says Nanak, between the faithful and the One, there is no
distinction.

8   *Truth is in their minds, Truth is on their lips.*
Except for the One, they see no other.
Says Nanak, these are the qualities of the enlightened.
1   The enlightened in this world are unattached,

Like the lotus in the pond, untouched by water.
The enlightened are without fault,
Like the sun free from all moisture.
The enlightened view everyone equally,
Like the air touching king and beggar alike.
The enlightened retain their poise,
Like the earth dug over or revered with sandal paste.
The enlightened maintain a steady temperament,
Says Nanak, like fire burning at its natural temperature.

2 The enlightened are the purest of the pure,
Like water never defiled by filth.
The minds of the enlightened are spread with light,
As the earth is spread with the sky.
The enlightened treat friend and foe alike,
The enlightened have no pride,
The enlightened are the highest of the high,
But in their humility they are the lowest of the low.
They alone become enlightened,
Says Nanak, who are inspired by the Divine Itself.

3 The enlightened see themselves as the dust of all people,
The enlightened see to the spiritual core,
The enlightened are kind to all,
The enlightened inflict no harm,
The enlightened view everyone alike,
The enlightened cast ambrosial glances,
The enlightened are free from all constraints,
The enlightened live in purity,
The enlightened make knowledge their food and drink,
Says Nanak, the enlightened are attuned to the Transcendent.

4   The enlightened regard the One as their only support,
The enlightened are immortal,
The enlightened are steeped in humility,
The enlightened delight in helping others,
The enlightened are free from all entanglements,
The enlightened still the flickering mind;
The enlightened act only for the good,
The enlightened reap the fruit of all their actions,
The enlightened liberate all who accompany them,
Says Nanak, the entire world exalts the enlightened.

5   The enlightened are suffused with the single hue,
The enlightened dwell with the One,
The enlightened have the Name as their refuge,
The enlightened have the Name as their family,
The enlightened are ever awake,
The enlightened discard their ego,
The enlightened enjoy supreme bliss,
The home of the enlightened is full of joy,
The enlightened live in peace and serenity,
Says Nanak, the enlightened are immortal.

6   The enlightened know the Transcendent,
The enlightened love only the One,
The enlightened are free from anxiety,
The enlightened follow a perfect mandate,
The enlightened are enlightened by the Divine Itself,
The enlightened are magnificent in their brilliance,
Blessed are they who see the enlightened.
To the enlightened we offer ourselves.
The great god Shiva seeks the enlightened.
Says Nanak, through the enlightened we find the
    Transcendent Itself.

7 The enlightened are beyond price,
They hold all creation in their mind.
Who can know the mystery of the enlightened?
Our salutations ever to them.
We cannot express a jot of their praise,
They truly are the protectors of all.
Who can express the limits of the enlightened?
Only the enlightened know their own state.
The enlightened are unfathomable and infinite,
Says Nanak, salutations ever to them.

8 The enlightened are the creators of the universe,
The enlightened live for ever, they are immortal,
The enlightened give us life, they show us the way to
   liberation,
The enlightened are perfect, the writers of our destiny,
The enlightened are the refuge of the homeless,
The enlightened extend their benevolent hand to all,
The enlightened possess the multiplicity of forms,
The enlightened themselves are formless,
Only the enlightened can express the glory of the enlightened,
Says Nanak, the enlightened are the rulers of all.

9 *They who embrace the Name in their hearts,*
Who envisage the One pervading all,
Who worship the Sovereign every moment,
Says Nanak, they are the purest, they free us all.

1 Those whose tongues do not utter a single lie,
Whose hearts long for a vision of the Immaculate One,
Whose eyes do not covet the wife of another,
Who serve the holy in the company of the faithful,
Whose ears do not listen for slander,

Who regard themselves as the lowest of all,
Who, by the grace of the Guru, tear the veil of illusion,
Who discard all desires from their mind,
Who conquer their senses and are free of the five passions,
Says Nanak, such pure people are one in a million.

2   Those who please the Divine One are true Vaishnavites,
They are separated from the world of illusion,
They are devoted to work but not to its fruit.
The faith of such Vaishnavites is truly sincere,
They have no desire for the fruit of their actions,
They are only immersed in songs of praise.
With mind and body they contemplate the Protector,
And they shower their grace upon all.
They contemplate the Name, they inspire others,
Says Nanak, such Vaishnavites attain the highest state.

3   Those who are dyed in the divine Colour are true Bhagavats,
They abandon all corrupt company,
They cast out all doubts from their mind,
Their hands ever worship the Transcendent.
In the company of the faithful, they wash away the filth
    of misdeeds,
The wisdom of such Bhagavats is heightened indeed.
They serve the Creator day and night,
With mind and body dedicated to loving the Divine.
In their heart they rest at the Feet of the Divine.
Says Nanak, such Bhagavats attain the Supreme One.

4   Those who awaken their minds are true pundits,
They seek the Name in their inmost self,
They drink the essence of the Name.
Taught by such pundits, the world comes alive.

In their hearts they cherish the divine Story,
Such Pandits never return to the cycle of birth.
They know the core of the Vedas, Puranas and Smritis,
They see the transcendent root of our phenomenal world,
They give their teaching to all four castes,
Says Nanak, salutations to these pundits for ever.

5   The essential formula gives knowledge to all,
The four castes are equally free to recite the Name.
Whoever recites It, is liberated,
But only some keep the company of the faithful.
Through grace, the Name reaches our inner self,
It liberates animals, ghosts, the ignorant, even the
    stony-hearted.
The Name heals all suffering,
The Name reveals mercy, joy, and exaltation.
We cannot find It through disciplined deeds or rituals,
Says Nanak, they alone find It who are blessed
    from the very beginning.

6   Those with minds that house the Transcendent,
They alone can be called the truly devout.
They see the Transcendent in their inmost self,
Through loving the faithful they reach their goal.
Always knowing the One is so very close,
They are warmly received in the Court.
The One showers gifts upon the attendants,
And they come to know all.
Living in joy, but free from attachment,
Says Nanak, such is the life of the truly devout.

7   Those who treasure the Decree in their inmost self,
They alone can be called free in this life.

Joy and sorrow are the same to them,
They live in constant bliss, they know no separation.
Gold and clay are the same for them,
Ambrosia and bitter poison,
    Glory and blame,
Pauper and king — all are the same for them.
Whatever may happen, they fully accept.
Says Nanak, we call such people free in this life.

8 All places belong to the Transcendent,
As You maintain them, so we define them.
All that happens is divinely decreed,
Whatever pleases You, that alone comes to be.
You Yourself have expanded Yourself in infinite waves,
No one can express the Emanation.
We are enlightened according to the wisdom You impart,
Our transcendent Creator is invincible.
You are always and always compassionate,
Says Nanak, remembering You brings us bliss.

10 *Countless devotees praise You, but none can fathom*
   Your vastness.
 Says Nanak, You created us in such diverse and infinite forms.

1 There have been countless devotees,
Countless worshippers performing rituals,
Countless pilgrims living at sacred sites,
Countless wanderers in forests,
Countless listeners to Vedic recitations,
Countless practitioners of austerities,
Countless meditators on their inner self,
Countless thinkers on sacred verse,

Countless reciters of Your ever new names,
And yet, says Nanak, none can plumb the depths of the
    Creator.

2   There are countless who are arrogant,
     Countless blindly ignorant,
     Countless mean and miserly,
     Countless cold and insensitive,
     Countless greedy for another's wealth,
     Countless slandering others,
     Countless busy gathering illusory joys,
     Countless wandering in foreign lands,
     We all do what You assign to us,
     Says Nanak, the Creator alone knows the mystery of creation.

3   There are countless siddhas, celibates and yogis,
     Countless kings and pleasure-seekers,
     Countless birds and reptiles,
     Countless stones and trees,
     Countless airs, waters and fires,
     Countless countries, lands and continents,
     Countless moons, suns and stars,
     Countless gods and demons, and their chiefs with parasols,
     The entire universe is perfectly beaded on Your thread.
     Says Nanak, those who please You are blessed.

4   There are countless types of passion, inertia and truth,
     Countless Vedas, Puranas, Smritis and Shastras,
     Countless oceans full of jewels,
     Countless species of creatures,
     Countless beings with long lives,
     Countless golden Mount Sumers,
     Countless guardians, centaurs and slaves,

Countless ghosts, pigs and lions.
You are close to us all and yet so far.
Says Nanak, You are within us all, and yet beyond our grasp.

5   Countless beings live in the underworld,
     Countless dwell in heaven and hell,
     Countless are born, live, and die,
     Countless migrate from life to life,
     Countless eat without doing a thing,
     Countless work themselves to death,
     Countless are made wealthy,
     Countless fret over fleeting delights,
     As You decree, so each is sustained,
     Says Nanak, everything is held in the divine Hand.

6   Countless are they who renounce the world,
     They are wrapped in the Name.
     Countless are they who seek the Transcendent,
     They search within their deepest self.
     Countless are they who thirst for the divine vision,
     They ultimately meet the invincible One.
     Countless are they who yearn for the company of the faithful,
     They bask in the divine radiance.
     They who are showered with Your joy,
     Says Nanak, are blessed for ever.

7   There are countless species, and countless continents,
     Countless skies, and countless constellations,
     Countless incarnations of deities who appear.
     In countless ways, the universe expands,
     At countless times, the universe unfolds,
     But the One exists forever —
          the single One Transcendent Being.

Countless creatures issue in countless forms,
From the One they emerge, into the One they converge.
No one knows Your vastness,
Says Nanak, only You, the Absolute Reality,
    can know Yourself.

8   Countless are those who are devoted to the Transcendent,
They are illuminated by the Light inside.
Countless are those who know the Essence,
Their eyes for ever see the One.
Countless are those who drink the ambrosial Name,
They become immortal, they live for ever.
Countless are those who glorify the Name,
They revel in joy and peace.
With every breath, You watch over Your devotees,
Says Nanak, they truly are loved by You.

11   *The Author of this creation is the Transcendent One,*
    there is no other.
    Says Nanak, I offer myself to That One who pervades
    the land and sea.

1   You are the Creator and the Cause,
All proceeds by Your Will,
In an instant You raise, in an instant You dissolve,
There are no limits to Your dimensions.
The world is supported by Your unsupported Will,
Every origin and end is in Your Will,
All good and bad actions depend on Your Will,
Countless colours and forms emerge from Your Will,
You create, and You oversee Your handiwork,
And yet, says Nanak, You remain within us all.

2   If You will, we humans attain bliss,
      If You will, stones can float,
      If You will, life survives without breath,
      If You will, we praise the Name,
      If You will, the fallen are exalted,
      You do whatever You think of doing,
      You are the Sovereign of this world and beyond,
      Your sport You enjoy, and You know our deepest self,
      We do only what You Will,
      Says Nanak, besides You, I see no other.

3   Tell us, what can we humans accomplish?
      We can do only what You will.
      Had we the choice, we would have grabbed it all,
      But we can do only what You will.
      The ignorant drown in poison,
      Had they wisdom, they would save themselves.
      Entranced by illusion, they run in all directions,
      In a flash, their minds flit across continents.
      They on whom You bestow Your devotion,
      Says Nanak, they alone merge in the Name.

4   In an instant, You can make a lowly worm king,
      Truly You are the champion of the poor.
      They who are unknown to all,
      At once become renowned the world over.
      They to whom You are kind
      Are not accountable to the Final Judge.
      Our life, our body is entirely Yours,
      Each of us is filled with Your bright Transcendence.
      You created Your own creation, Creator,
      Says Nanak, I live only to witness Your grandeur.

5   We have no power in our hands.
     You, Sovereign, are our Creator, our Supreme Cause,
     We are merely obedient, we follow Your Will,
     Your Will alone comes to pass.
     At times we are noble, at times we are base,
     Now we suffer in pain, now we laugh in joy,
     We slander, and we worry,
     We rise sky high, we sink to the underworld,
     But at times we are enlightened, and contemplate
          the Transcendent.
     Says Nanak, You Yourself unite us with Your Self.

6   At times we dance in different ways,
     At times we sleep both night and day,
     At times we are full of terrible wrath,
     At times we are humble as dust,
     At times we act as great kings,
     At times we act as lowly beggars
     At times we end in dishonour,
     At times we land with honour,
     We live as You design,
     By the grace of the Guru, I speak the truth, says Nanak.

7   At times we are scholars, discoursing out loud,
     At times we are meditators, wrapped in silence,
     At times we are pilgrims, bathing at sacred banks,
     At times we are ascetics, seekers and instructors,
     At times we are worms, elephants and moths.
     Circling and straying in countless lives,
     Just as a mimic appears in different forms,
     So goes our dance, according to Your Will.
     Whatever pleases You, comes to pass.
     Says Nanak, there is no other.

8 When we are blessed in the company of the faithful,
There is no more turning,
Inside we are lit with wisdom,
A state that has no end.
Mind and body have only one Colour,
And we abide for ever in the company of the Transcendent.
As water merges with water,
So our light merges with the Light.
The cycles of migration end, and we find peace.
Says Nanak, I for ever offer myself to the Divine.

12 *The humble live peacefully, they are free from their egos,*
The mighty, the haughty, says Nanak, they rot in their pride.

1 They who are proud of their royal blood,
End living like dogs in hell.
They who are proud of their youth,
End living like worms in dirt.
They who are proud of their good fortune,
End migrating from one life to another.
They who are proud of their land and wealth,
Are blind and ignorant fools.
They whom You graciously give the gift of humility,
Says Nanak, are liberated here, they live peacefully hereafter.

2 The rich are proud of their riches,
But not a straw goes with them at death.
Some may rely on their armies and soldiers,
But in an instant their forces are destroyed.
Some regard themselves as the mightiest,
But in a flash they are reduced to ashes.
In their conceit, some think themselves unaccountable,

But at the last, they are chastened by the Final Judge
They who let go of their pride, through the grace
    of the Guru,
Says Nanak, they are accepted in the Court.

3   Countless good deeds done with conceit
Bring exhaustion, they come to nothing.
Countless sacrifices proudly performed
Return us to birth, to the cycle of heavens and hells.
If countless efforts do not subdue the self,
How can we enter the Court?
They who call themselves good,
Goodness does not approach.
They who become humble as dust,
Says Nanak, they are perfectly glorious.

4   While we think that we legislate,
We find no peace.
While we think that we execute,
We migrate from womb to womb.
While we judge others as enemies or friends
We do not find stability of mind.
While we are lost in the fantasy of love and delight,
We are punished by the Final Judge.
Through divine favour, our bonds are broken.
Says Nanak, by the grace of the Guru, our ego is dispelled.

5   Earning thousands, we chase millions,
In pursuit of wealth, we are never content.
Countless hollow delights beguile us,
But discontented, we die in pain.
Without contentment, we are never fulfilled,
Like vapid dreams, our goals and efforts are in vain.

The Name, the Deliverer of radiant joy,
The most fortunate alone receive.
You Yourself are the Creator, You the Cause,
Says Nanak, forever recite the Name.

6   You are the Creator, You are the Cause and the Agent,
Let us consider what is in our control.
We are designed by Your favour,
You Yourself are the Absolute One,
From Your Radiance we are produced,
You dwell afar and yet so close to each and all.
You see, You recognize, and You reason,
You Yourself are the One, You Yourself are the many,
You are immortal and invincible,
You are never born, You never die,
Says Nanak, You are forever present in us.

7   You are the source of instruction, You are its recipient,
You are with everyone,
You extend Your own vastness,
Everything belongs to You, the Creator of all,
Nothing is apart from You,
You permeate all land and space,
You conduct Your own sport,
How wondrous are Your infinite workings.
You are in us, and we in You,
Says Nanak, how priceless is this treasure.

8   True, true, true is our Sovereign,
Seen only by the Guru's grace.
True, true, true is Creation,
One in a million recognize this.
Blessed, blessed, blessed is Your Form,

So beautiful, boundless, and unmatched.
Perfect, perfect, perfect is Your Word,
It resonates within, It resounds on every tongue.
Pure, pure, utterly pure are they,
Says Nanak, who recite the Name with love.

13 *They who take shelter in the faithful find ultimate liberation*
They who denigrate the faithful migrate from birth to birth
again and again.

1 Offending the faithful, our lifespan shortens,
Offending the faithful, we succumb to the god of death,
Offending the faithful, our comfort departs,
Offending the faithful, we end in hell,
Offending the faithful, our thoughts corrupt,
Offending the faithful, we lose our stature,
Struck by the faithful, there is no protection,
Offending the faithful, our space is desecrated,
When the benevolent faithful grant their grace,
Says Nanak, even the corrupt are liberated with them.

2 Offending the faithful, our faces distort,
Offending the faithful, we caw like crows,
Offending the faithful, we take rebirth as snakes,
Offending the faithful, we crawl like worms,
Offending the faithful, we seethe with desire,
Offending the faithful, we cheat everyone,
Offending the faithful, we lose our radiance,
Offending the faithful, we sink lower than the low,
Offending the faithful, we are left without shelter
But, says Nanak, if the faithful so please, even the offenders
are saved.

213

3 Slanderers of the faithful are the most offensive,
  Slanderers of the faithful are without a moment's rest,
  Slanderers of the faithful are brute murderers,
  Slanderers of the faithful are punished by the Supreme,
  Slanderers of the faithful have no power,
  Slanderers of the faithful live in pain and poverty,
  Slanderers of the faithful suffer from many diseases,
  Slanderers of the faithful are always alienated,
  Slandering the faithful is the vilest offence,
  But says, Nanak, if the faithful so please, even the slanderers
   are liberated.

4 Offenders of the faithful are always impure,
  Offenders of the faithful are nobody's friend,
  Offenders of the faithful are soon punished,
  Offenders of the faithful are shunned by all,
  Offenders of the faithful are full of pride,
  Offenders of the faithful live corruptly,
  Offenders of the faithful revolve in transmigration,
  Offence against the faithful casts out peace,
  Offenders of the faithful have no refuge,
  But, says Nanak, if the faithful so please, even the offenders
   attain union.

5 Offenders of the faithful are left in mid-air,
  Offenders of the faithful have nothing complete,
  Offenders of the faithful wander in the wilderness,
  Offenders of the faithful stray from the straight path;
  Offenders of the faithful are hollow inside
  Like a corpse without breath.
  Offenders of the faithful have no roots,
  For what is sown, that alone is reaped.
  Offenders of the faithful have no other protector,

But, says Nanak, if the faithful so please, even the offenders
are delivered.

6   Offenders of the faithful lament,
    As a fish out of water writhes in pain.
    Offenders of the faithful are never satisfied,
    As fire devours wood and rages for more.
    Offenders of the faithful are left alone,
    As burnt weeds lie abandoned in the field.
    Offenders of the faithful cast righteous action away.
    Offenders of the faithful speak only lies.
    The deeds of the offenders are written from the Beginning,
    Says Nanak, whatever pleases You, that comes to pass.

7   Offenders of the faithful grow deformed,
    Offenders of the faithful are punished in the Court,
    Offenders of the faithful forever gasp with thirst,
    Offenders of the faithful are neither alive nor dead,
    Offenders of the faithful have unfulfilled dreams,
    Offenders of the faithful depart from this world in despair,
    Offenders of the faithful do not find peace.
    As You will, so we become,
    Your destined deed cannot be undone.
    Says Nanak, only the True One knows.

8   All our bodies are Yours, Creator,
    Our salutations to You for ever.
    Sing praise of the Divine night and day,
    Remember the One with every breath, every bite you take,
    All happens according to Your Decree,
    As You design, so we become.
    The cosmos is Your sport and You are the player,
    Who else could think it out?

They whom You favour receive the gift of Your Name,
Says Nanak, they indeed are most fortunate.

14 *Good people, give up all cleverness,*
and contemplate the Divine.
Nurture desire only for the One, so, says Nanak,
our suffering, doubt, and fear are undone.

1 Realize how worthless is human support,
There is only one Giver — the Transcendent One.
We are replete with the gifts we receive,
And thirst no longer.
The One alone destroys and creates,
We humans hold nothing in our hands.
To follow that Command brings peace,
So, wear the necklace, beaded with the Name,
Remember, remember, remember the One,
Thus, says Nanak, no obstacles block our path.

2 Exalt the Formless One within,
Mind, be forever in commerce with Truth,
Tongue, drink the ambrosial nectar,
Life, be forever peaceful,
Eyes, behold the divine Radiance.
In the company of the faithful, all others disperse.
Feet, walk towards our Protector.
A little meditation cancels all misdeeds.
Hands, do good; ears, hear the Word.
Says Nanak, so may our foreheads shine in the Divine Court.

3 Blessed in this life
Are they who forever sing praise of the Divine.
They who reflect upon the Name

Are rich and powerful in this world.
They who recite the Divine with their mind, body and tongue
Are always and always the most peaceful.
They who recognize the One, the absolutely single One,
Understand the here and hereafter.
They whose minds are bathed in love for the Name,
Says Nanak, they know the Immaculate One.

4   They who, by the grace of the Guru, discover their self
Are quenched of desire.
They who exalt the Divine in the company of the faithful
Are set free from all disease.
They who sing songs of praise night and day
Find sacred bliss in married life.
They who centre their hopes on the One alone
Are freed from the snare of death.
They who hunger for the Transcendent,
Says Nanak, their suffering is stilled.

5   They who hold the Divine in their mind
Are ever faithful, they never waver.
They who are blessed by the Divine,
Why should those devotees fear another?
The perfection of the Absolute is revealed to them
Permeating the many forms.
Through searching and reflecting, our efforts bear fruit,
By the grace of the Guru, we discern the Centre.
Whichever way we turn, we see our Source,
Says Nanak, the One has form, and yet the One is formless.

6   Nothing is ever born nor does it ever die,
It is simply Your sport, and Your play.
All comings and goings, all things seen and unseen,

Truly, the entire creation — everything — follows Your Will.
You are the Absolute Reality, pervading all,
You devise and dissolve in so many ways,
You are invincible, You are immutable,
You have the whole universe under Your command.
Ineffable and unfathomable is Your splendour,
If You will, says Nanak, we may contemplate You.

7   They who know the Divine are honourable,
Through their teaching, the world is delivered.
The devotees of the Divine save us all,
The devotees of the Divine dispel our suffering.
You graciously unite them with Yourself,
By reciting the Word, they are blessed.
Those on whom You bestow good fortune,
They in turn serve Your devotees.
By contemplating the Name, we find peace,
Says Nanak, honour such people as supreme.

8   All their actions shine with divine Radiance,
Always and always, they dwell with the One,
Every event is natural to them,
For they recognize its ultimate Designer.
Divine action is sweet for them,
They see things as they truly are.
They unite with their Source,
The prize is peace.
How You reciprocate their honour,
Says Nanak, between You and Your devotees,
no difference lies.

15 *You are all-powerful, You are all-knowing,*
We are saved by contemplating You, says Nanak,

I offer myself to You.

1   You mend our broken ties,
You sustain us,
You cherish us,
No one is without You,
May my mind always contemplate You.
You are immutable, You are the Absolute Reality,
Nothing happens of our accord.
Though we may strive a hundredfold,
Without You, nothing avails.
Says Nanak, we find liberation only by remembering You.

2   Why should the beautiful be attached to their selves?
It is Your Light which adorns all bodies.
Why should the wealthy be vain?
It is Your wealth that endows them.
Why should some be called mighty heroes?
Without Your power, they would not move.
When we regard ourselves as munificent,
Our Giver knows how crude we are.
Those who are cured of ego by the grace of the Guru,
Says Nanak, are always healthy.

3   As a building rests on pillars,
So our mind is sustained by the Guru's Word.
As a stone is carried in a boat,
So we are liberated by holding on to the Guru's feet.
As a lamp shines light into darkness,
So we are elated by a vision of the Guru.
As a path is found in the jungle,
So we are enlightened by the company of the faithful.
I seek to follow the faithful,

Says Nanak, please fulfil my wish.

4   My foolish mind, why do you weep?
We obtain what was ordained for us.
Suffering and joy come from the One,
So abandon all else, and contemplate the One.
Whatever happens, accept with joy,
Why are you lost, my ignorant fool?
Did anything come with you at birth?
So why do you cling like a greedy moth?
By remembering the One in our hearts,
We enter our Home in honour, says Nanak.

5   We came to buy treasure in this world —
The Name, found in the home of the faithful.
Bartering away our pride, we must purchase our self,
And weigh the Name in the scales of our heart.
Loaded with this freight, we must travel with the faithful,
Casting aside all poisonous entanglements.
Whoever meets us calls us blessed,
And with glowing faces, we enter the Court.
Very rare are they who engage in this trade,
Says Nanak, I offer myself to them.

6   Let us wash the feet of the faithful,
And dedicate our lives to them.
Let us bathe in the dust from their feet,
And offer ourselves to them.
Fortunate are they who serve the faithful,
Together let us sing praise of the Divine.
The faithful protect us from many dangers,
And we taste the ambrosial nectar by singing Divine praise.
Seeking the shelter of the faithful,

I have come to their portal, says Nanak, and I have won
   perfect joy.

7   The dead are granted life,
    The hungry are given sustenance,
    Your vision is bountiful,
    We obtain what was ordained for us.
    All things belong to You, You are their Creator,
    There has been no other but You, nor will there ever be.
    Let us always remember You day and night,
    This is the highest and purest of deeds.
    They who are graciously given the Name,
    Says Nanak, they become pure.

8   They who place their trust in the Guru,
    The Divine One enters their consciousness.
    Their devotion is renowned in every land,
    Their hearts are immersed in the single One.
    Their action is Truth, Truth their life,
    Truth is in their hearts, Truth is on their lips
    Truth is their sight, Truth their form,
    Truth is their way, Truth their revelation.
    They who discern the Transcendent as Truth,
    Says Nanak, they themselves merge with Truth.

16 *You have no form, no feature, no colour.*
      You are apart from the three strands of the universe.
    Says Nanak, they who please You
      are the ones who discern You.

1   We must keep the Immortal inside ourselves,
    And discard our attachment to mortals.

There is no one beyond the Transcendent,
And That One abides immutably in all.
You are the Seer, You are the Knower,
You are unfathomable, deep, profound and wise,
You are transcendent, our supreme Being, our
  True Sovereign,
You are the Treasury of compassion, kindness
  and forgiveness.
May I be devoted to Your faithful,
Says Nanak, this is my heart's desire.

2 Fulfiller of our wishes! Our worthy protector!
   What You write on our palms always comes to pass.
   All creation and dissolution are a blink of Your eye,
   But no other knows Your Mystery.
   You are the embodiment of bliss — all joys lie in You;
   You are the precious Treasury — all things are stored
     with You.
   You are the Ruler of rulers, Yogi of yogis,
   You are the Ascetic of ascetics, part of the family.
   By contemplating You, Your devotees win peace,
   Says Nanak, no one has found the extent of Your Being.

3 There is no limit to Your sport,
   Gods have given up their search in vain,
   For how can the child know the birth of its parent?
   The entire universe is beaded on Your thread.
   They to whom You impart wisdom, knowledge and
     contemplation
   Are Your devotees, they recite Your Name.
   They who are deluded by the three strands of the world
   Migrate from one birth to another.
   High and low, all belong to You,

Says Nanak, what You will, that is what we know.

4   You have countless forms, You have countless colours
     You have countless guises, yet You are One.
     You have designed Your expanse in countless styles,
     Yet You are eternal, transcendent, the singular Being.
     You put on myriad shows in a flash,
     Yet you are completely present everywhere.
     You have created the world in countless ways,
     Yet You alone know Your own worth.
     All hearts are Yours, all places Yours,
     Says Nanak, we live only to recite Your Name.

5   Your Name is the ground of all beings,
     Your Name is the ground of all continents and constellations,
     Your Name is the ground of all Smritis, Vedas and Puranas,
     Your Name is the ground of all hearing, knowledge and
         contemplation,
     Your Name is the ground of all earths and skies,
     Your Name is the ground of all forms,
     Your Name is the ground of all spheres and universes,
     All are liberated by hearing Your Name.
     They who, through Your gifts, follow Your Name,
     Says Nanak, they attain the highest state.

6   Your form is Truth, and True is Your seat,
     You are the True Being, our sole Sovereign,
     Your actions are True, and Truth is Your Word,
     Your True Being is present in us all.
     Your works are True, Your creation is True,
     When the Source is True, Its output is Truth.
     Purest of the pure are Your doings,
     They who are enlightened see good in all.

Your True Name brings us joy and peace.
Says Nanak, from the Guru we gain our trust in Truth.

7   The faithful teach us Truth,
When it settles in us, we also become True.
Those who understand the love of Truth
Recite the Name, and they are freed.
You are Truth, Your creation is Truth,
You alone know Your own dimensions.
The universe belongs to You, You are its Creator,
No other can know it, no matter their speculations.
How can the created know their Creator?
Says Nanak, only what You will comes to pass.

8   We are awed by Your marvels,
Those who see savour the boundless joy.
Your devotees are flooded with Your brilliance,
And, by the Guru's Word, they attain the four goals of life.
They freely give, and they rid us of suffering,
By their presence the world is saved.
They who serve them are fortunate indeed,
For in their company everyone is wrapped in You.
They who sing praise of the Ultimate Protector
Says Nanak, reap the fruit by the grace of the Guru.

17   *Truth before time. Truth thoughout time.*
Truth here and now. Says Nanak, Truth is evermore.

1   Your Feet are true, and true are those who touch them,
Worship of You is true, and true are those who serve You,
Vision of You is true, and true are those who see it,
Your Name is true, and true are those who reflect upon it.

You are Truth, and true is Your creation;
You are Virtue, and You are one with the virtuous.
Your Word is true, and true are those who recite it,
Your Revelation is true, and true are those who hear
    Your Glory.
They who know Truth, become true,
Says Nanak, You are Truth, absolute Truth!

2   Those who realize the Truthful One in their hearts
Recognize the Source of all Creation.
They who entrust their hearts to the Divine
Have minds that are lit with the essence of knowledge.
Freed from anxiety, they live fearlessly,
They unite with their very Source.
When particular merges with its universal type,
Who can tell them apart?
This the wise and insightful discern.
Says Nanak, by meeting the One, we become One.

3   Your devotees are at Your command,
Your devotees attend You for ever,
Your devotees trust fully in You,
Your devotees live a pure life.
They know You are near them,
They shine with the radiance of Your Name.
Your devotees are nurtured by You.
Formless One, Your devotees are protected by You.
They who receive Your mercy, are Your devotees,
Says Nanak, and they remember You with every breath.

4   You cover the failings of Your devotees,
You maintain their honour,
You bestow glory on Your devotees,

And they recite the Name.
You Yourself keep up their esteem,
But none can see Your limits.
We cannot match the greatness of Your devotees,
For they are the highest of the high.
They who are inspired to serve You,
Says Nanak, are world-renowned.

5   A tiny ant empowered by You,
Can reduce a million armies to ashes.
Those whose lives You do not wish to end,
You guard with Your own Hand.
We humans try so many ways,
But all our efforts go to waste,
No other can preserve or destroy,
You alone are our Saviour.
Why then do we worry?
Says Nanak, just remember the ineffable and wondrous One.

6   Let us remember the Divine again and again,
Quench mind and body with the ambrosial nectar.
They who obtain the Jewel of Name
See nothing else.
The Name is their wealth, the Name their beauty and joy,
The Name is their comfort, the Name
    their constant company
They who drink the essence of the Name
Have mind and body fully immersed in it.
Awake, sitting or asleep, they are wrapped in Your Name,
Says Nanak, this is Your devotees' undying aim.

7   Let us recite Your glory day and night,
Our power to praise is Your gift to us.

In our devotion and with deep joy,
We merge completely with You.
Our past and our present, we accept,
Knowing them as Your ordinance.
How can we express Your grandeur?
We cannot gauge a single virtue.
They who dwell in Your presence night and day,
Says Nanak, are fulfilled in their life.

8   My mind, seek their shelter,
Let us dedicate our minds and bodies
To those who recognize their Sovereign,
For they are truly the treasury of all gifts.
In their shelter, we find peace,
In their sight, suffering ends.
Discard all cleverness,
Serve them instead,
Then will we cease to come and go.
Says Nanak, always pay homage to them.

18   They who realize the True Being,
*   their name is the True Guru.*
In their company, Sikhs are liberated.
*   Says Nanak, let us sing divine praise.*

1   The True Guru protects the Sikhs,
The Guru is ever giving to the devotees,
The Guru washes away the impurities of their mind,
By the Guru's Word the Name is exalted.
The True Guru sunders all bonds,
The Guru's Sikhs turn away from evil,
The True Guru grants the gift of the Name,

The Guru's Sikhs are so fortunate.
The True Guru blesses the Sikhs here and in the hereafter.
Says Nanak, the True Guru remembers the Sikhs with life.

2   Devotees who dwell in the home of the Guru
Must bear this mandate in their minds:
Don't take credit for your actions,
Always and always remember the Name.
By selling their mind to the Guru,
All their tasks are fulfilled.
By serving with no desire for gain,
They find their Sovereign.
They who are granted Your compassion,
Says Nanak, they accept the Guru's instruction.

3   The devotees who fully please the Guru,
Know the vastness of the Transcendent.
To the True Guru who is wrapped in the Name,
I offer myself countless times.
This Guru is a treasury of all gifts,
Dyed in divine brilliance, day and night.
The Ultimate is in the individual, the individual
is in the Ultimate,
The two are one, there is no duality.
A thousand clever feats will not enlighten us,
Says Nanak, only by good fortune is the Guru found.

4   Seeing the Guru brings meaning and purity,
Touching the Guru's feet arouses the good in us,
Entering the Guru's presence inspires us to sing divine praise,
It grants us access to the Court.
Hearing the Guru's Word calms our ears,
Our mind becomes content, our spirit refined.

Perfect is the Guru, immutable the message,
They who receive the Guru's ambrosial sight become
    like saints.
Endowed with countless virtues, the Guru cannot be
    appraised,
Says Nanak, those who please the Guru obtain divine union.

5   How can our one tongue ever recite Your infinite praise?
You are the True Being, Absolute Intelligence.
What language can lead us to You?
You are unfathomable, unknown, ever serene.
You take no food, You are without enmity, and You always
    bring us joy.
None can appraise Your value.
Countless devotees pay You homage
With hearts steeped in love for You.
We offer ourselves a hundred times to the Guru,
Says Nanak, whose grace enables us to praise the Divine.

6   Few are they who savour the Divine essence,
Who drink the ambrosial nectar and become immortal.
They are never destroyed,
For their minds glow with the treasury of virtues.
Day and night they remember the Divine
And they impart true instruction to the devotees.
Mock delights cannot sway them,
For their minds are absorbed only in the One.
As a light of the lamp expels darkness,
Says Nanak, these rare ones dispel all doubt, attachment
    and suffering.

7   In scorching heat we are cooled,
Bliss is found, all suffering is annulled.

Fear of birth and death is erased,
All through the teachings of the faithful.
We live fearlessly, for fear departs,
We live peacefully, for all ailments depart,
We receive grace from the One to Whom we belong,
In the company of the faithful we recite Divine Praise.
We are freed from dualities and the cycles of transmigration,
Says Nanak, by hearing the glory of the Divine.

8   Totally transcendent and yet so palpable,
The Formless One takes on forms and enchants us all.
Creating Your own sports,
You alone know Your worth.
You are the sole Reality,
Invariably pervading us all.
On Your pattern and colour, the universe is woven,
Yet we recognize You only in the company of the faithful.
You uphold Your creation by Your own strength,
Says Nanak, I offer myself to You countless times.

19 *We turn to ashes.*
So earn the Name, says Nanak, this is our lasting wealth.

1   Reflect in the company of the faithful,
Remember the One, and draw strength from Its Name.
My friends, abandon all other efforts,
Plant the lotus feet deeply in your heart.
Our Creator, our Primal Cause is almighty,
Hold firmly the object of the Name.
Gather this wealth, and enjoy true fortune,
For this is the true teaching of the faithful.
Nurture only one desire,

Says Nanak, so that our maladies are dispelled.

2   The wealth we chase in every direction,
We receive by serving the Divine.
The comfort for which we are always thirsting,
We receive by loving the faithful.
The glory we seek in noble deeds,
We receive by contemplating the One.
The sickness for which countless remedies are tried,
We cure with the medicine of Divine praise.
The Name is the Treasure of treasures,
Says Nanak, by reciting it, we are received in the Court.

3   Through the Name we are enlightened,
Our craving for everything ends, peace is found.
The way of life is smooth and clear,
For those whose hearts are filled with the One.
The present age is blistering hot, the Name is refreshingly
    cool,
Through contemplation we find joy for ever.
Fear is dispelled, our hopes fulfilled,
Our inner self shines bright with devotion,
So we make our way to the home of the Eternal One.
Says Nanak, we are freed from the snare of death.

4   Those who consider and discuss Reality are true humans,
False are they who merely live and die.
By serving the One we break the cycle of birth and death,
Casting our ego aside, we take shelter in the Guru.
Thus our precious human life is fulfilled,
We remember the One, the Source of every breath.
Countless efforts will never liberate us,
Nor studying various ancient texts.

Only by loving devotion to the Divine,
Says Nanak, are all our hopes fulfilled.

5   None of these riches follows us at death,
Then why be drowned in them, foolish mind?
Amongst children, friends, family and wives,
Who will be our ultimate support?
Fettered by power and worldly delights,
How can we be delivered?
Horses, elephants and sumptuous chariots,
False are they, and false is their display.
But, ignorant mind, do we know their Producer?
Says Nanak, when we forget the One, we end in regret.

6   My ignorant mind, follow the Guru's teaching,
Without devotion, many clever people have failed.
My friend, love the Divine,
For that is how refinement is acquired.
By imprinting the lotus feet in our mind,
The vices from past lives are erased.
Let us remember the Name and remind others as well,
By hearing, reciting and living the Name, we are liberated.
The Name is the essence, the form and the reality;
Says Nanak, let us praise the Name spontaneously.

7   Singing of divine glory washes away filth,
And the fast-spreading poison of the ego is destroyed.
We live in peace and serenity if we remember the One,
With every breath we take, and every morsel we eat.
Cast aside all other cleverness, my mind,
And earn true wealth in the company of the faithful.
Engage in the true trade, and accumulate the divine Treasure,
Thus we find peace here and glory in the hereafter.

They regard everybody as equal, without distinction,
Says Nanak, they whose foreheads shine with good fortune
   from before.

8   Remember the One, exalt the One,
     Contemplate the One, desire only the One,
     Sing the infinite praises of the One,
     Immerse mind and body in the Supreme One.
     There is only the One, the One alone is real
     The Absolute One is suffused in all,
     Infinite expanses flow from the One,
     And by recalling the One, evil is cast away.
     The One radiates through our body and mind.
     Says Nanak, we recognize the One by the grace of the Guru.

20   *After wandering all around, I have come to You.*
     Says Nanak, it is my wish. May I always be devoted to You.

1   We beggars beg from You, our Sovereign.
     Grant us the gift of Your Name.
     We wish to serve Your devotees,
     Fulfil our wish, my Transcendent.
     May we always recite Your praise,
     Remember You with every breath.
     May we worship Your lotus feet,
     Love You night and day.
     You are our sole support, You are our only shelter.
     Says Nanak, I seek Your Name — the essence of all.

2   The sight of the Divine bestows bliss,
     Rare are they who are blessed with it.
     They who drink the divine essence are fulfilled,
     They attain perfection, they never falter again.

They are deliciously filled with sweet love,
Surging with joy, in the company of the faithful.
With You as their shelter, they abandon all else,
Wrapped in You, they glow day and night.
Blessed are they who contemplate the Divine
Says Nanak, steeped in Your Name, we find bliss.

3   The desires of the devotees are fulfilled,
With the guidance of the True Guru.
The One graciously bestows favours,
The devotees are showered by eternal joy.
Bonds are severed, and freedom found,
Birth, death, suffering, all dualities come to an end,
Wishes are granted, and faith fulfilled,
With the Divine shining brightly in all.
From whence we emerge, into That we merge,
Says Nanak, through devotion we are absorbed in the Name.

4   Why forget who rewards our efforts?
Why forget who knows all our actions?
Why forget who gives us everything?
Why forget who blesses us with life?
Why forget who sustains us in the womb?
Through the grace of the Guru, just one in a million
    understands.
Why forget who frees us from deadly illusions?
Why forget who reunites broken ties?
The essence of the Guru's teaching,
Says Nanak, is to remember the Transcendent.

5   My good friends, follow my advice,
Discard all else, and contemplate the Name.
Remembering the Name, we find peace and joy,

So let us contemplate and help others as well.
By loving devotion we cross the fleeting world,
But without that devotion we end in ashes.
The treasury of the Name contains all peace and joy,
It extends a life-line to the drowning.
The Name ends all suffering,
Says Nanak, remember this treasury of virtues.

6   Love and joy arise within,
Mind and body are ecstatic.
The vision of the One brings peace,
The mind blossoms in the company of the faithful.
The devotees shine in body and mind,
Rare are they who join their company.
Have compassion and bestow one gift:
By the grace of the Guru, may we contemplate Your Name.
You are beyond compare,
Says Nanak, You are ever present in us all.

7   The One is compassionate and giving,
Beloved of the devotees, ever gracious,
Shelter of the homeless, Protector of the earth,
Present in all, sustaining all.
Creator, You are the Primal Being,
    You are our Primal Cause.
You are the very life of Your devotees.
They who contemplate You become pure,
For they are deeply in love with You.
We are worthless, base and ignorant,
Says Nanak, we seek Your shelter, Supreme One.

8   They who exalt You even for a moment
Reach paradise and liberation.

Great power, glory, and pleasure abound
In the telling of the Name.
The joys of delicious food, silk and music abound
In the constant recitation of the Name.
Morality, honour and wealth belong
To those whose hearts carry the full teaching of the Guru.
May we abide in the company of the faithful,
Says Nanak, all joys are thus revealed to us.

21 *Formless One, You are both unseen and seen, You are the*
   Primal Silence.
   Having created everything, says Nanak, You reflect upon Your
   creation.

1   When all that we see was not yet created,
     Where then was good and evil?
     When You were still in primal silence,
     Where then was any antithesis?
     When there was no shape or colour,
     Who then felt joy or sorrow?
     When all that existed was the Transcendent,
     Where then was attachment or duality?
     You created Your sport, and You are the Player,
     Says Nanak, You are the Doer, there is no other.

2   When You alone were the owner,
     Who could be deemed bound or free?
     When the inscrutable and infinite One alone existed,
     Where then were heaven, hell or incarnations?
     When the Formless was present alone,
     Where then were the forms of Shiva and Shakti?[5]

---

[5] The divine representations of masculine and feminine power. See Glossary.

236

When You alone were shining in Your light,
Who then was fearlesss? Who then quaked in fear?
You perform Your own wonders,
Says Nanak, You are our inscrutable infinite Ruler.

3   When You sat peacefully on Your throne, Eternal One,
Where then were birth, death or dissolution?
When You the all-perfect Creator were all by Yourself,
Who then could fear death?
When You were the only One — ineffable and inscrutable —
Whose records could be questioned by the messengers
      of death?
When You alone existed, our immaculate inscrutable Ruler,
Who then was liberated? Who then was in bondage?
You Yourself are the absolute Wonder of wonders,
Says Nanak, You Yourself reveal Your own Self.

4   When You alone existed, my Sovereign Immaculate One,
Where was impurity? What had to be cleansed?
When all was the immaculate, infinite One in bliss,
Who was honoured? Who dishonoured?
When the only form was the Sovereign alone,
Who then could be blamed with deceit or misdeeds?
When all was You — Your own light merged with light,
Who then was hungry? Who satisfied?
You are the Creator, the Maker, the Primal Cause,
Says Nanak, we can never fathom Your limits.

5   When You were absorbed in Your own radiance,
Where then were mother, father, friend, son and brother?
When You, our Ultimate Wisdom, alone existed,
Who then reflected on any scriptures of East or West?
When You abided in Your very own heart,

What then could have been ominous or auspicious?
When You Yourself were high above, You Yourself
    deep down,
Who then could be called owner or slave?
We are awed by Your marvels,
Says Nanak, You alone know Your own extent.

6   When there was only the invincible, invulnerable One,
Who then could be enticed by the illusory world?
When You greeted but Your Own Self,
The three strands of the world were not yet present.
When there was the One, only the absolute One,
Who could then be carefree or worried?
When You were content in Yourself,
Who then spoke? Who would have heard?
You are infinite, the Highest of the high,
Says Nanak, Your limits You alone can reach.

7   When You formed the phenomenal world
Its three strands expanded.
It was then that evil and good appeared
And the notions of heaven and hell.
It was then that the visible world spread its snares,
Deceiving with ego, attachment, duality, fear.
It was then that suffering, joy, respect and dishonour
Were spread abroad in different ways.
All is Your sport which You eagerly watch,
Says Nanak, when the play is over, the One alone remains.

8   Wherever the Formless One is, the devotees are there,
But the phenomenal world is also formed for the fame
    of the faithful.
You are the ruler of the here and hereafter

Your glory You alone can appraise.
You are the creator of all wonders and delights,
And You delight in them, transcendent though You are.
They who please You, You inspire with Your Name
They who please You, You engage in Your sport
You are infinite and immeasurable
Says Nanak, I speak only as You command.

22   *You are our Ruler, and You dwell in us too.*
Says Nanak, only the One exists, we see no other.

1   You are the speaker, You are the listener too,
     You are both the Single One and the Infinite Expanse.
     When You Will, creation is formed,
     By Your Will, it is dissolved.
     Without You, nothing comes to pass,
     Our whole cosmos rests as a bead on Your thread.
     Only they whom You enlighten recognize You,
     They receive the True Name,
     Wise to Your Essence, they see everyone alike,
     Says Nanak, they triumph throughout the world.

2   All life is held in Your control,
     You champion the poor and forlorn.
     Those You protect, no one can harm,
     But those You neglect are instantly destroyed.
     Abandoning You, where do we go?
     Formless One, You are our sole support.
     The workings of the universe are driven by Your Hand,
     Within and without, You are ever with us.
     The infinite Transcendent is full of virtue,
     Says Nanak, I offer myself to You forever.

3   Compassionate One, perfectly present,
     You bless everyone,
     You know Your own affairs,
     And the secrets of every heart.
     You nurture life in varied ways,
     Those You create, meditate upon You,
     They who please You are united to You,
     They love You, they sing Your praise,
     Their minds are filled with faith,
     Says Nanak, they trust their single Creator.

4   Your devotees are devoted to Your Name,
     May their wishes never be in vain.
     The faithful will serve for ever,
     They discern Your Will, they earn the highest bliss.
     Absorbed in the Formless One,
     They think of no other.
     Free from bondage, free from hate,
     They worship You night and day.
     They are happy in this life and beyond,
     Says Nanak, You grant them union with Yourself.

5   Let us celebrate in the company of the faithful,
     Recite songs of transcendent joy,
     Reflect upon divine Glory,
     Recover our precious body.
     To sing the ambrosial Word
     Is our ultimate goal.
     To know You near by day and night
     Dispels darkness and ignorance from our life.
     Keeping divine Instruction in our heart,
     Says Nanak, we win the fruit of all our desires.

6   We are exalted in the here and hereafter,
If we wear the Name in our heart.
The perfect Instruction by the perfect Guru
Shows our minds the ultimate Truth.
In mind and body, devoted to the Name,
We dispel all fear and suffering.
Let us be traders in the business of Truth,
This product alone will take us to the true Court.
If we focus on our sole Support,
Says Nanak, we return to birth no more.

7   To whom can we turn apart from You?
We live only by remembering You.
Fearless One, Your remembrance banishes fear,
Your compassion brings us freedom.
There is no suffering for those You sustain,
All joy is won by contemplating Your Name.
Anxiety and pride depart for ever,
No rival can ever match us.
When the Almighty stands above us,
Says Nanak, all our deeds are perfected.

8   The embodiment of wisdom and ambrosia,
Our whole cosmos is liberated by Your sight.
Your lotus feet are beyond compare,
Your beautiful form brings fulfilment to all.
Blessed is Your devotion, blessed Your devotees,
You the Almighty are intimate with every heart.
They who contemplate You are exalted,
Death cannot touch them,
They are immortal, they win eternity,
Says Nanak, in the company of the faithful,
    we remember You.

23   *They to whom the Guru gives the eyeliner of wisdom,*
        their dark ignorance disappears.
     Through grace, we meet the faithful, says Nanak, our mind is
        enlightened.

1   Amidst the faithful, we discover the One within,
      And we taste the delicious Name.
      The vibrant and diverse cosmos
      We see existing in Your single heart.
      Your ambrosial Name embracing all treasures
      Dwells in our very body.
      We hear the unstruck melody within,
      We experience ineffable joy within.
      Only they whom You enlighten see You,
      Says Nanak, they are fully knowing.

2   The One within is the infinite, transcendent One without,
      You are in us all,
      Earth, sky, underworld
      And all galaxies are nourished by You.
      Forests, grass, mountains are You, Transcendent,
      And everyone obeys Your command.
      You are in air, water and fire,
      And in the four quarters, and in the ten directions.
      There is no space devoid of You.
      Says Nanak, we find bliss by the grace of the Guru.

3   Behold the One in the Vedas, Puranas and Smritis.
      In the moon, sun and constellations that very One abides.
      Everyone speaks Your Word in various tongues,
      While You stay immutable in all.
      You create all forms, You play Your own sports,
      We can never assess the value of Your virtues.

All creatures are informed by Your light,
All are grounded in You.
By the grace of the Guru, all doubts are erased,
Says Nanak, we have faith only in You.

4   The faithful see the Divine everywhere,
     The faithful clasp morality to their hearts,
     The faithful hear only good words,
     They are absorbed in the all-pervading One.
     This is the way of life of those who know,
     And the faithful say only what is true.
     Whatever happens they accept happily,
     For they know the ultimate Creator and Cause.
     The One exists inside us, the One exists outside us,
     Says Nanak, we are enchanted by Your presence.

5   You are Truth, You created Truth,
     All creation is from You.
     If You Will, You expand into diversity,
     If You Will, You are the One Being.
     We cannot express Your infinite powers.
     They whom You please, You unite with Yourself.
     Who can we say are near to You? Who far?
     You, You Yourself are everywhere.
     Those whom You grant inner wisdom,
     Says Nanak, they see into their essence.

6   You exist in every creature,
     You are the sight of all who see.
     The whole cosmos is Your body,
     You are the praise, You are its audience.
     You designed this game of come and go,
     This world of flux obeys Your Will.

At the centre of all beings, ever transcendent, You remain.
Whatever is said is spoken by You.
We come by Your Will, we go by Your Will,
Says Nanak, we merge with You if You will.

7   Your deeds are never in vain,
We do nothing without You.
You are goodness itself, and so are Your deeds,
Only You can know Your inner workings.
You are Truth, You created Truth alone,
The whole cosmos is woven into You.
Your dimensions no one can tell,
For who but an equal could measure You?
Your actions we fully accept,
Says Nanak, such assent comes by the grace of the Guru.

8   Those who recognize You are always in bliss,
You unite them with Yourself.
They enjoy true wealth, noble birth and honour,
With You in their hearts, they are free in this world.
Blessed, blessed is their birth,
For they bring freedom to the world by their grace.
The goal of their life is to inspire their companions
To contemplate the Name.
Free themselves, they bring freedom to the world,
Says Nanak, my homage to them for ever.

24   *We revere the Absolute, whose Name is absolute too.*
Says Nanak, we win the Absolute, if we sing the praise
of that Absolute.

1   Listen to the teaching of the Absolute Guru,
Let us see the Transcendent intimately within us.

Let us remember the Protector with every breath,
So shall our worries depart.
Let us discard our desires rolling like waves,
Let us yearn for the company of the faithful.
Abandoning our ego, let us pray
That we swim across the ocean of fiery waves.
Let us fill our treasury with the Name,
Says Nanak, my homage to the Absolute Guru.

2   As we remember the Transcendent with the faithful,
Comfort, peace and eternal bliss are ours,
Hell is evaded, life redeemed,
We sing divine praise, and we drink the ambrosial nectar.
Our mind contemplates the Supreme One,
The Formless One of so many different colours.
Preserver of all, compassionate of the lowly,
You annul our suffering, our absolute and beneficent One.
Let us remember Your Name again and again,
Says Nanak, for this is our only support.

3   The words of the faithful are glorious,
They are jewels most precious.
Listening to them and abiding by them,
We liberate ourselves and we liberate others.
They whose minds are suffused with radiance,
Are triumphant, triumphant are their friends.
They who resonate with the unstruck melody,
Hear the One, they enjoy supreme bliss,
Their foreheads shine with revelation,
Says Nanak, we too are liberated by their presence.

4   Hearing of You as our Refuge, we have come to You,
Have compassion on us, that we may unite with You.

We have expelled hate, we welcome humility,
In the company of the faithful,
    we sing Your ambrosial Name.
By pleasing You, our supreme Guru,
The devotion of Your devotees is fully fulfilled.
We are freed from all entanglements and vice
As we hear Your Name and recite Your praise.
Through compassion, You bestow Your grace,
Says Nanak, so we profit in our trade.

5   My good friends, let us sing divine praise,
       With single mind, ever alert.
       The pearls of peace shine on the thread of the Name,
       Those who wear them are treasuries of wealth,
       All their desires are fulfilled,
       They are exalted and celebrated through all the worlds,
       They win the highest station,
       Are subject to birth and death no more.
       Only they who receive your gifts,
       Says Nanak, walk away with the sacred wealth.

6   Comfort, peace, riches, the nine treasures,
       Intelligence, wisdom, the various miraculous powers,
       The merit of knowledge, austerity, penance and
          contemplation,
       Of supreme discernment, and most sacred ablution,
       Life with its four goals, the self ever blossoming like a lotus,
       Living in the midst of all yet free from all constraints,
       Beauty, cleverness, insight into the essence,
       An equal regard for everyone —
       All these fruits are garnered by those,
       Says Nanak, who recite and hear the Name.

7   Few recite this precious treasure within,
     They live freely in all ages,
     Their speech resounds with the praise of the Name,
     As Smritis, Shastras and Vedas have declared.
     The Name is the omega of all faiths,
     Dwelling in the mind of the faithful.
     The company of the faithful dispels countless faults,
     Their grace saves us from the snare of death.
     Those whose foreheads shine with the divine gift,
     Says Nanak, they alone seek the company of the faithful.

8   They who cherish this treasure within,
        who hear it lovingly,
     They remember the Divine constantly.
     Freed from the suffering of life and death,
     Their precious body is instantly liberated.
     Their fame is unblemished, their words ambrosial,
     For the One Name pervades them.
     Suffering, sickness, fear and duality depart,
     They are known as the faithful, all their actions are good.
     They receive the highest glory.
     No wonder, says Nanak,
        the Name is the pearl of peace — *sukhmani.*

The Ten Sikh Gurus

First	Guru Nanak	1469-1539
Second	Guru Angad	1504-52 (Guru 1539-52)
Third	Guru Amar Das	1479-1574 (Guru 1552-74)
Fourth	Guru Ram Das	1534-81 (Guru 1574-81)
Fifth	Guru Arjan	1563-1606 (Guru 1581-1606)
Sixth	Guru Hargobind	1595-1644 (Guru 1606-44)
Seventh	Guru Har Rai	1630-61 (Guru 1644-61)
Eighth	Guru Har Krishan	1656-64 (Guru 1661-4)
Ninth	Guru Tegh Bahadur	1621-75 (Guru 1664-75)
Tenth	Guru Gobind Singh	1666-1708 (Guru 1675-1708)

Contributors to the Guru Granth

The Guru Granth was compiled by the Fifth Guru and includes selections of his own and the earlier Sikh Gurus' works as well as those of Hindu and Muslim saints. The Tenth Guru later added poetry by his father, the Ninth Guru. His own works were compiled separately in the Dasam Granth.

Sikh Gurus

First, Guru Nanak: 974 hymns
Second, Guru Angad: 62 couplets
Third, Guru Amar Das: 907 hymns
Fourth, Guru Ram Das: 679 hymns
Fifth, Guru Arjan: 2218 hymns
Ninth, Guru Tegh Bahadur: 59 hymns and 56 couplers

Bhaktas (Hindu) and Sufis (Muslim)

Kabir: 292 hymns
Farid: 4 hymns and 130 couplets
Namdev: 60 hymns
Ravidas: 41 hymns
Jaidev: 2 hymns
Beni: 3 hymns
Trilochan: 4 hymns
Parmananda: 1 hymn
Sadhana: 1 hymn
Ramananda: 1 hymn
Dhanna: 4 hymns
Pipa: 1 hymn
Sain: 1 hymn

Bhikhan: 2 hymns
Sur Das: 2 hymns
Sundar: 1 hymn
Mardana: 3 couplets
Satta and Balvand: 1 hymn
Bhatts: 123 swaiyyas

Glossary of Terms and Phrases

Bar, the. The region between the Beas and Ravi rivers.

Bhagavat. The "Blessed" or "Adored". It refers to those involved in the popular spiritual practice of adoration of God.

Brahma. In the cosmic cycle of creation, preservation and destruction, Brahma is the creator god. Vishnu and Shiva are respectively the preserver and destroyer gods.

Buddha. In the classical language of India, "the Enlightened". A general term as well as specific reference to Siddhartha Gotama, the historical Buddha.

Chatrik. Also known as the "rain bird" because of its call which heralds the rains.

Dharmaraja. God of Judgment.

Dhru. Indian sage and pole star. Also Dhruva.

Five beloved ones. The first five initiates into the Khalsa. Also the five Khalsa Sikhs who conduct initiation ceremonies.

Five elements. Water, fire, earth, air and ether.

Forty who obtained liberation. Forty Sikhs who deserted Guru Gobind Singh but later returned, died in battle and were forgiven by the Guru and declared to have attained liberation.

Four and forty. See *Four princes* and *Forty who obtained liberation.*

Four elements. Earth, air, fire, water.

Four princes. The four martyred sons of Guru Gobind Singh.

Four goals of life. Dharma (morality), artha (material gain), kama (sensual pleasure) and moksha (ultimate release).

Four sources of life. Blood and/or sperm, egg, sweat and earth, traditionally believed to be the progenitors of new life.

Fourteen worlds. One of the Indian cosmologies for referring to the entire universe.

Gopi. Cowherd girl. Usually associated with the Indian god Krishna who danced with and made love to them. The gopis are understood to represent all humanity.

Gunas. See *Three gunas.*

Gurudwara. Literally, a door, dwara, to ultimate enlightenment, guru. It refers to the building which enshrines the Guru Granth and is also the centre of community life. Also spelt gurdwara. For further details, see "From Guru Nanak to the Guru Granth", pp. 31-3.

Kateb. Scriptures of the Middle East.

Khalsa. The Sikh Order of Purity, open to women and men, constituted by Guru Gobind Singh in 1699; see pp. 28-9.

Khalsaji. Respectful address to the Khalsa.

Koel. Indian cuckoo. Its cry is believed to stimulate tender yearning in the hearer.

Krishna. An avatar of the god Vishnu, and one of the most popular figures in the Indian pantheon. The lover and playmate of humanity.

Laxmi. Goddess of fortune and prosperity and consort of Vishnu, god of preservation.

Nankana Sahib. Birthplace of Guru Nanak, now in Pakistan.

Nath. Member of the ascetic tradition of India which espoused Hatha-yoga, a tantric system of rigorous bodily purification exercises, as the means to spiritual liberation.

Nine treasures. Categorisarion embracing all the treasures in the world.

Parvati. The mother goddess. Also known as Shakti, Durga and Kali, the latter two with particular reference to the dark, destructive aspect of feminine power. She is the consort of Shiva the destroyer god and, like him, is associated with the Himalayas.

Pir. Muslim holy teacher.

Pundit. Hindu religious scholar.

Puranas. Hindu tales and legends.

Qadi. Judge in Islamic law court.

Qur'an. Sacred text of Islam.

Rag. The different melodic frameworks which are used in Indian music as the basis of improvisation. Different rags are associated with particular times of the day, seasons and moods.

Rahim. The Compassionate One. One of the ninety-nine Names of Allah.

Rama. An avatar of the god Vishnu and one of the great warrior kings of Indian folk history, the hero of the much-loved epic, the *Ramayana.* Rama represents ideal man in roles such as father, son, brother, husband, king. His wife is Sita, the ideal woman (see below).

Ravana. The demon opponent of Rama in the *Ramayana.*

Sachi's husband. Indra, the sky god.

Shakti. Mother goddess, feminine power. See Parvati.

Shastras. Hindu sacred writings.

Shiva. In the cosmic cycle of creation, preservation and destruction, Shiva is the destroyer god. Brahma and Vishnu are respectively the creator and preserver gods.

Siddha. "Perfect One". Specifically a famed group of eighty-four tantric saints but also used as a more general term.

Sita. An avatar of the goddess Laxmi, consort of Vishnu. As Sita she is the wife of Rama and represents the ideal woman in roles such as wife, mother, daughter.

Six doctrines, six philosophies, six traditional schools. Six schools of orthodox Indian thought, recognized by the brahmins as roads to salvation. They respectively espoused: (1) the essential oneness of all existence; (2) Vedic rituals; (3) logic; (4) an atomized universe of soul, mind, time and space; (5) a dualistic atheistic universe in which the spirit is entangled in matter; and (6) a dualistic world in which physical discipline and meditation on an immortal god lead to repatriation in the spiritual realm. In practical terms these schools form a general pool of philosophy which informs a multitude of cults and traditions.

Sixty-eight pilgrimage sites. Categorisation used to signify all pilgrimage sites.

Smritis. Hindu sacred writings with particular reference to those that are "remembered" as opposed to "heard" or revealed.

Swayamvara rites. Ceremony in which a girl chooses her husband from a number of assembled suitors.

Takhts. The five seats of Sikh temporal authority. They are the Akal Takht in Amritsar, Patna Sahib in Bihar, Keshgarh in Anandpur, Hazur Sahib in Nander near Hyderabad, and Damdama Sahib near Bhatinda. Sikhs see them as places from which decisions are made about their faith.

Ten directions. The eight compass points plus up and down.

Ten gifts. Categorisation used to signify the divine gifts of existence.

Three gunas. The three natures or qualities of which all existence partakes to varying degrees: sattva, peace and light, represented by white; rajas, activity and passion, represented by red; and tamas, inertia and ignorance, represented by black. The ways in which these combine determines a person's personality.

Three strands. See *Three gunas.*

Three worlds. Heaven, earth and underworld.

Vaishnavite. Followers of the god Vishnu, one of the most popular Hindu traditions.

Vishnu. In the cosmic cycle of creation, preservation and destruction, Vishnu is the preserver god. Brahma and Shiva are respectively the creator and destroyer gods.

Vedas. The ancient and foundational scriptures of Hinduism.

Yogi. Spiritual practitioner. Related to the English word "yoke", with connotations of both work and union.

Select Bibliography

Readers wishing to further their understanding of Sikh beliefs, values, practices and history may find the following books useful.

Overview and History

Cole, W. Owen and Sambhi, Piara Singh, *The Sikhs: Their Religious Beliefs and Practices.* Sussex Academic Press, Brighton, 1995.

Grewal, J.S., *The Sikhs of the Punjab.* Cambridge University Press, 1990.

Macauliffe, M.A., *The Sikh Religion.* Oxford University Press, India, 1909. Reprint 1985 in three volumes.

Sikhism: Its Ideals and Institutions. Orient Longman, Calcutta, 1964.

Singh, Gopal, *A History of the Sikh People 1468-1988.* World Book Centre, New Delhi, 1990.

Singh, Harbans, *Guru Nanak and Origins of the Sikh Faith.* Publication Bureau, Punjabi University, Patiala, 1994.

Singh, Harbans, *The Heritage of the Sikhs.* Manohar, India, 1994.

Singh, Khushwant, *History of the Sikhs* (2 vols). Oxford University Press, 1991.

Textual

W. H. McLeod, *Textual Sources for the Study of Sikhism.* Manchester University Press. Reprint Chicago, 1990.

Sikhs in the West

Barrier, N.G. and V.A. Dusenbury (ed), *The Sikh Diaspora*. Chanakya Publications, Delhi, 1989.

Singh, Darshan, *Western Perspective on the Sikh Tradition*. Sehgal, New Delhi, 1991.

Sikhism and Feminism

Singh, Nikky-Guninder Kaur, *The Feminine Principle in the Sikh Vision of the Transcendent*. Cambridge University Press, 1993.

Directories

Shergill, N.S., *International Directory of Gurdwaras and Sikh Organisations*. 1986. Available from Virdee Brothers, 102 The Green, Southall, Middlesex, England UB2 4BQ.

Religions in the UK: A Multifaith Directory. 1993. Published by and available from the University of Derby, Mickleover, Derby, DE3 5EX, England.

The Golden Temple

Singh, Patwant, *The Golden Temple*. ET Publishing Limited, Hong Kong, 1988.